Children in Groups

CHILDREN IN GROUPS

A Social Work Perspective

Marian F. Fatout

AUBURN HOUSE
Westport, Connecticut • London

Library of Congress Cataloging-in-Publication Data

Fatout, Marian F.
    Children in groups : a social work perspective / Marian F. Fatout.
        p.   cm.
    Includes bibliographical references and index.
    ISBN 0–86569–256–4 (alk. paper)
    1. Social work with children.   2. Social group work.   I. Title.
    HV713.F27   1996
    362.7—dc20   95–34263

British Library Cataloguing in Publication Data is available.

Library of Congress Catalog Card Number: 95–34263
ISBN: 0–86569–256–4

First published in 1996

Auburn House, 88 Post Road West, Westport, CT 06881
An imprint of Greenwood Publishing Group, Inc.

Printed in the United States of America

The paper used in this book complies with the
Permanent Paper Standard issued by the National
Information Standards Organization (Z39.48–1984)

10 9 8 7 6 5 4 3 2 1

Contents

Preface

Groups have existed from the beginning of time in the form of clans, tribes and families. These units of people joined together to help each other and to accomplish tasks that were important to their well-being. Over many years, society has continued to recognize, understand and refine the many contributions that groups can make to both the community and to individuals. The use of groups with adults has long been a method for providing therapeutic assistance when needed.

During the Industrial Revolution in America, there was a proliferation of groups for children that were intended to build character, educate and preserve the way of life. As groups were used in a variety of settings, there was recognition of their real potential in affecting the lives of children.

As child guidance clinics developed, the focus for help initially was the parent of the child having problems. As a result, parents were counseled about how to help their children. With time, there also began to be recognition of some of the contributions that groups could make in working directly with children.

Literature and research focused on groups for adults have continued to grow, but there has been little recognition and focus on groups for children. By the 1970s, a few individuals had begun to make a plea for the recognition of work with children as a specialized area of practice. It was believed that it was important to establish a beginning foundation for the definition, knowledge base and methods for service in this area.

Because of this recognition of need for the development of a foundation of knowledge and practice wisdom focused on children, this book was born. Theories about working with groups have been developed and utilized for adults, and reference is often made to how the specifics might be differentially applied to children, but very little literature and attention has been focused solely on children.

The nature of much of the group work with children in the beginning was focused on helping them to retain their previous way of life and to grow into healthy human beings. Groups such as Girl Scouts and Boy Scouts were usually conducted by well-meaning volunteers. Most groups and volunteers were not prepared to work with children who already had serious problems.

Groups have been found to be helpful to children in a variety of ways including prevention, assisting with development tasks and rehabilitation. Groups have the potential of turning things around in a child's life; however, this does not happen automatically. It is only with the careful guidance of a purposeful, knowledgeable, skilled and caring adult(s) that positive outcomes can be more assured.

With the many upheavals in society today, and the often scarcity of time of parents and other family members, it is important for all adults to give help and support to children. The often-heard slogan is, "It takes a village to raise a child." This statement has been overused, perhaps, but the meaning remains as important as ever.

This book focuses on some of the basic knowledge essential for helping professionals who intend to work with children in groups. There is emphasis on knowledge about groups, with application of current ideas and concepts as applied to groups of children. The other major focus area is that of child development of the school-age child. A combination of this information is woven into the discussion of many other concepts and ideas throughout the book.

OVERVIEW OF THE BOOK

The book begins with an overview of some of the earliest group work with children, focused on the theory of groups and child development. This is followed by material that emphasizes the processes and dynamics required to assist the child to change, develop and grow in a positive manner. This latter material is interwoven with recognition of group stages and the many developmental needs of the children as well as examples intended to illustrate the points made.

OUTLINE OF THE BOOK

This book is divided into two parts. Part I consists of two chapters focused on the two areas of theory essential to the practice of social work with children in groups. Chapter 1 reviews some of the historical development of group work with children and a description of current theory about working with groups of adults. Next some application of these theories are translated and applied to children's groups, specifically in the area of knowledge about stages of group development.

Chapter 2 describes the transition of the child into the middle years and the dynamics and growth that are occurring. The areas discussed and applied are the psychological state, physical growth, cognitive development and sexual and social development.

Part II consists of seven chapters (Chapters 3–9) that describe the development and uses of the group for working with children. Chapter 3 focuses on the planning essential to forming a purposeful group, with attention to the many factors that can be expected to impact on the group's success. After this has been accomplished and the children come together, a major task for the worker is to develop a mutual aid system which allows members to be helpful to each other; this is identified and elaborated on in Chapter 4.

Chapters 5 and 6 describe some of the most essential change processes used in working with children. Chapter 5 describes the major procedure and techniques used in working with groups. Then a specific procedure using structure and limits, which has been found especially useful in working with children, is described and illustrated.

Chapter 6 identifies and illustrates the variety of play and activity and how they are utilized in children's groups. The differing types of play are described, and emphasis is placed on fitting play to the specific problem in order to help children work on and resolve some of their issues.

In Chapter 7, elements of group process are described, noting changes that might be expected throughout the life of the group. This knowledge is useful for the worker, and sometimes the group, to note. It helps gain a better sense of the group's current stage and aspects of the process that may need to be changed in order to enhance the functioning of the group and its members.

In groups, the individual members as well as the whole system are very important to accomplishment of goals. Chapter 8 describes the need to individualize and work with each member toward his/her own personal goals. Conferences both in and outside the group are used for this purpose and are illustrated in this chapter. Conferences with parents, families and collaterals are also discussed.

Chapter 9 focuses on ending groups. Because endings and the manner in which they are accomplished are so important to stabilizing the gains already made, it was believed that a chapter elaborating on this stage was essential. Highlighted is the need to help members move through this process, to allow children to work through feelings, to evaluate gains and regrets and to move on. The workers, too, need to prepare for endings by being self-aware and evaluating their own work with the group and the members in preparation for helping children move through this process.

Acknowledgments

I wish to acknowledge the ongoing support of Dr. James Midgley, former Dean of the School of Social Work at Louisiana State University, and current Associate Vice-Chancellor of Research and Economic Development at LSU. He has continued to offer help and assistance as needed. A major contributor to the idea for this book is Dr. Helen Northen, Professor Emeritus, School of Social Work, University of Southern California. She recognized the need for a book of this type and encouraged me to write it.

I also wish to thank the colleagues, students and especially the children who have provided opportunities for me to learn and grow along with them.

PART I

THEORETICAL UNDERPINNINGS

Chapter 1

The Status of Group Work with Children

Group work with children is embedded in the historical development of the social work profession. Several of the early programs and agencies were focused on work with children. So called "character building" programs, such as Boy Scouts, Girl Scouts, Camp Fire Girls, Young Men's Christian Association and Young Women's Christian Association were all a part of this early history. Group work with children also played an important part in other organizations, such as settlement houses, camp vacation programs, brotherhoods like Jewish community centers and the Young Men's and Women's Hebrew Association, and recreational programs (Alissi, 1980; Fatout, 1992; Schwartz, 1971b; Wilson, 1976). Literature suggests that the purpose of these groups was often to educate, "build character" and preserve the way of life for children that existed before the chaos resulting from the Industrial Revolution.

After a time, work was not always focused directly on the children but rather on changing the environment for the protection of children. It was at this time that the Children's Bureau was established in the U.S. Department of Labor to "investigate and report . . . upon all matters pertaining to the welfare of children and child life among all classes of our people" (Coll, 1970, p. 49).

Early *treatment* of children developed almost unnoticed by the profession as a whole. Child guidance clinics were established throughout the country, with the focus of service on working with parents. The intent was to help parents learn how to work with the child who was perceived as having problems.

As the practice of group work with children expanded, it included children with a wide variety of problems or needs, including mental health and physical health, often growing out of poverty and dysfunctional family situations. As early as 1938, Gisela Konopka was working at the Pittsburgh Guidance Center with children. Fritz Redl's Detroit Project (Redl, 1944) was occurring in the early 1940s. The emphasis in these programs was on group work with children. This interest continued to grow and expand and has remained a major component of social work with groups.

SOCIAL WORK THEORIES FOR WORKING WITH GROUPS

Over time, many theories and theoretical approaches have emerged regarding working with groups, and numerous models (psychosocial, mediating, developmental, organizational, problem-solving, functional, task-centered, socialization and crisis intervention) have been identified (Roberts & Northen, 1976).

Almost without exception, all age groups are assumed to be included in operationalizing these theories. The practitioner working with children must determine the priority to be given to specific aspects of a theory in order to work with a particular client group. Some practitioners advocate that theories of social work specific to working with children be explicated. Hinchman (1977), after analyzing clinical practice with children and youths, concluded that "since it is generally felt that work with children in non-institutional mental health and family service settings is considered a specialized area of practice, establishing a beginning foundation for the definition, as well as knowledge base for services is essential" (pp. 7–8). In his analysis, Hinchman did identify ultimate values that are basic to all practice "but of special importance in working with children" (pp. 219–221) as follows:

1. The worth and dignity of all individuals is a primary concern of all social work.

2. There should be the opportunity for maximum realization of each individual's potential for development *throughout* his/her lifetime.

3. There are human needs common to each person, yet each person is essentially *unique and different* from others.

4. In addition to developing services to meet immediate needs, society has to create services geared to social betterment and social development.

5. Reactive intervention cannot take the place of prevention.

6. All values of the profession should be applied with consideration given non-adults as well as adults.

An Approach for Working with Children in Groups

Recognizing the need for theory development focused on work with children is, in itself, an important first step in the development of more precise practice methodology attuned to the specific needs and problems of children. In working with groups of children, an essential component of the knowledge base is some understanding of how the theories of group development are operationalized and used.

First, in order to understand children and their behavior in the group, it is essential to have some awareness of the duration of the group, the specific stage the group has reached and the progress that each child has made. The meaning underlying a particular child's behavior in the first session may be entirely different from the meaning behind the same behavior in a later stage of group development, therefore producing a different response from the worker than from other members.

For example, in the first session of a group, Tommie stated, "I don't want to play any games." The practitioner responded to the underlying meaning, believing that this is an assertive little boy who wants attention, has oppositional tendencies or is testing the limits. If, on the other hand, this child made same statement in the fifteenth session of a thirty-session group, and he had not ever asserted his desires previously, the response would be very different. There might even be cheers and certainly behaviors on the part of the worker that would be very supportive of this child's new behavior. The underlying meaning might be that Tommie has gained self-esteem, has learned to assert himself and has made some positive steps.

As noted earlier, many theories have developed about group phases or stages, but relatively little effort has been given to apply this material to work with children. Generally as group development is discussed, its application to work with children is woven into the total content being discussed. An example of this practice wisdom regarding a group of children in the beginning stage is, "children want to set rules for their groups, sometimes more rigid ones than they are able to follow and sometimes quite realistic ones" (Northen, 1988, p. 210). Levine (1979), too, has carefully noted some differences in the application of this area of theory to working with children. His major contribution is the recognition that children, because of their level of psychosocial development, may not attain the same level of inclusion as adults, which is expected to affect the depth of the later stages of group development.

These stages of group development have some characteristics that are similar to those of the developmental stages of the life cycle, especially those stages describing the development of a child (Erikson, 1963). One point of resemblance is that there may be some overlap between phases; that is, some group members may have moved on to the next stage, while others are still in the previous stage. It is essential that the tasks in each phase be accomplished before the group can move on satisfactorily. If members do progress to the next stage without fully accomplishing the necessary work to be done, it can be expected that their present group phase will have less depth than would ordinarily be anticipated. They can be expected to relate to each other in a more surface manner; to not have developed the depth of feeling and caring for each other, the group and the worker; and to be unable to progress in these areas to any great degree in the future.

With any upset in the steady state, the group or a portion of it may regress to the previous stage of group development. Often, this lasts for only a short time before the group returns to the level at which it had been functioning previously. Any number of situations may cause this to occur, such as the addition of a new member, the group being canceled for a session, the presence of a guest or sometimes the crisis in the life of a member outside the group.

An integrated model of group developmental stages was explicated by Northen (1988), which takes into account the paradigms developed by fifteen social work authors. Northen concluded, "Although there is always some distortion of reality in attempts to integrate and combine findings from diverse sources, certain trends seem to emerge from the major studies of the literature" (p. 177). These common trends will be utilized in developing and applying the material to work with children.

DEVELOPMENTAL STAGES IN CHILDREN'S GROUPS

Stages that deal with very comparable issues in each of the phases can be identified in working with children. Since four stages are most commonly used to represent the processes in the group, this model will be limited to four phases. The emphasis, focus and behaviors of the members and workers that characterize each stage, however, may be quite different from those of adult groups. The terminology used to identify these phases in children's groups will be as descriptive as possible of the process that is occurring, as children might view it. The descriptive content of each phase will take into account five areas of consideration. To gain a broader view of this area of knowledge, it is important: (1) to be aware of the primary issues to be resolved (both individual and group); (2) to note the emotions and behaviors of the members in working through the issues; (3) to be aware of the content of the discussions and/ or behaviors; (4) to understand the essential tasks to be accomplished by the group as a whole and by the individual members; and (5) to focus on the worker's behaviors and emotions that are useful in helping the group and the members complete the tasks.

"Getting Acquainted"

Stage I. This generally involves getting acquainted with each other, the worker, the environment and group expectations. In the beginning, a primary issue for the children is getting oriented to the group. They are concerned about their relationships with the other children and the worker. Focus is on themselves, and they are uneasy about being accepted by others in the group. They are likely to be anxious and concerned about what will happen in the group and what will be expected from them in order to participate. Initially, the children usually present themselves using their best behavior, often referred to by the workers as the "honeymoon period."

Other frequent feelings experienced by the children are excitement and anticipation regarding a new experience, uncertainty, distrust, tension and self-consciousness. Often, children attempt to bolster their uncertainty by reaching out to the worker for acceptance. This may occur as the children arrive for the session and compete with others for a seat as close to the worker as possible, sometimes on his/her lap. At the same time, other children may move as far away from the worker as possible, often while still seeking a connection. For the child who moves away from close contact with the worker, this "beginning to relate" is accomplished by eye contact or purposeful lack of contact. The child may look down or away from the worker until it is noted and becomes a concern to the social worker. Such behavior can be expected to cause the practitioner to pay special attention to this child and thus becomes a viable coping skill for the child and useful in establishing a relationship. The child may continue to use this game of making or withdrawing eye contact as a basis for establishing and maintaining a relationship with the leader.

During this early period of the group, discussions are likely to be scattered and brief, with a great deal of focus on self, "me" and "my." If toys, games or other program materials are available, children usually will become very stimulated and excited. Their interest in each item, however, is very short-lived, as they rush through the varied objects and touch, handle and talk about them.

Usually the first few sessions also include an exploration of the physical environment, especially if the children are meeting in an unfamiliar location. They often look into closets and cabinets, try buttons and electrical switches and generally become acquainted with their surroundings. This interest and exploration usually extends to the environment immediately outside the meeting room and may involve other workers, secretaries and personnel who are in close proximity. Generally, this exploration of external environment occurs as the members come to the session or after they leave their session.

Another important area of orientation for the child is that of developing relationships with peers within the group. Since there may be no psychological bond between the children in the beginning, the interplay and social exchanges that occur will result in the development of affective ties and communication. Both negative and positive relationships may emerge from this interaction. It is only as this process occurs and a group develops that the children are viewed as members. In the beginning, they act as an aggregate of individuals, later as members of a group. The child on entering a new group scans the situation to determine whether he/she is welcome. Only after receiving some positive signals does the child dare to explore further.

Behaviors can often be identified that clearly indicate that this scanning and exploration is occurring. An overt example of this was evident as a neighborhood group was being formed:

The worker had identified potential members for the group and had conducted individual interviews with them. Carmen met with the worker and seemed to be enthused that the group was to be formed. But when the worker clarified the time and place of the first session, Carmen made it very clear that she was not joining the group. Because the children lived in relatively close proximity and some went to school together, a few of them knew each other.

At the first session, however, Carmen was the second or third child to arrive. The worker, who was standing outside the door, greeted her enthusiastically and indicated that she was pleased that she had changed her mind about attending. Carmen smiled, picked up a stool and placed it in the doorway to the room, where she sat until everyone had arrived and entered the room. Because of Carmen's position, each child had to relate to her in some way. The general attitude conveyed by the others to Carmen was one of acceptance and positive feelings. As the group began, Carmen indicated that she could not attend this session, but if the worker would contact her mother she would be here next time. She had suffered many rejections by others and needed special evidence both from the worker and her peers that she was really going to be accepted.

Most children come to the first session and more discreetly test the situation for signs of acceptance or rejection by others. Often these messages are nonverbal, communicated by gestures, facial expressions and tone of voice. Latency age children, who are still learning ways to communicate and relate to peers, are perhaps more open to testing the meanings and consequences of not always heeding the messages that they are receiving. In addition, there is often a great desire to be in the group and to gain new exciting experiences.

This ambivalence often results in the child remaining for a few sessions to further evaluate his/her desire to be in the group. It is during this stage of group development that the membership begins to coalesce. Initially, the factors that influence the decision to remain in the group are

(1) the child's perception of the personal and social characteristics of the others; (2) his/her own psychosocial development and its fit with those of the group; (3) the content of the sessions and plans for future activities; (4) the reputation of the social agency in the community; and (5) cultural attitudes regarding the use of institutional resources.

Several essential tasks must be accomplished before the group and individuals are able to move on to the next stage. A primary concern is *trust*, of the worker and each other. Some practitioners suggest that this initial trust begins with the pre-group interview(s) with the worker and continues to develop as the group comes together. In this way, the relationship with the worker becomes a bridge for membership in the group. This initial affective bonding with the worker is then expanded to include others.

In order to aid the children in gaining trust and developing a readiness to move on to the next stage, there are certain worker behaviors that are useful in this process. First, the purpose of the group as identified in individual interviews should be repeated, explored and clarified. This sameness of content from the first contact with the worker to the present time helps to promote beginning trust of the worker and the situation. The expectations regarding the role of the worker and the members must be discussed and agreed upon. Confidentiality and behavioral limits must be discussed and settled. Some discussion of norms and values is also essential. Children may be involved in making a few broad rules for their group. This type of activity helps the group begin to develop some sense of "oneness" or beginning cohesion.

Another important focus for the worker is the need to respond to the members in ways that permit and enable them individually and as a group to move on to the next stage. It is important to allow some distance between individuals, both psychologically and in the use of physical space. There must be opportunities and worker support for the individuals to explore the setting and parameters; situations must be made available that invite trust, perhaps facilitated by program or the use of other similar structure.

The most basic tasks for the worker are to begin to establish relationships between the members, to enhance motivation to participate and ultimately to create a group with its own culture and potential for providing help for the members.

In order for the group to move on to the next stage, certain changes need to have occurred. As interaction between members continues, communication is established and patterns of relationships evolve. There is some initial (though weak and fragile) cohesion. There is some agreement concerning the purpose of the group, and norms and values have begun to develop. It is during this period that each child is attempting to determine whether he/she really wants to become a part of this group.

"Establishing My Place in the Group"

Stage II. Once the members have decided to remain in the group, the patterns of relationships between them become more of the issue. It is during this phase that there may be struggles over power and control that result in conflict and hostility. The areas of focus are communication patterns, status rating, rebellion, autonomy and issues of permission and normative crisis. Testing becomes a primary behavior. In the previous stage, members explored the parameters of behavior and environment. Now, children often begin to actively test the limits.

The behaviors of the members during this time are flocking, fighting, feeling and, for some, fleeing. Relationships between the members are worked out; for those who do not find a place, there is withdrawal. During this phase, children often begin to question a variety of dimensions of the group experience. They may express unhappiness with the structure and organization of the group, the timing, the worker, expectations of the group and the authority and power distribution. Questions may be posed such as "Why can't we meet on Saturday instead of Mondays?"; "Why can't Mr. Mike be our leader?"; or "Why can't we play all the time in here instead of sitting down to talk?"

The children are likely to express a great deal of frustration, anger, discouragement, anxiety, competitiveness, hostility and disappointment. When these questions arise, as often as possible the group should be involved in a decision-making process to resolve them. (There are some instances where changes cannot be made, and the worker needs to let the members know that the agency's or worker's schedule does not allow for another time, place or worker.) In areas where it can be functional, the decision-making process is very useful in helping the members work through some of the issues involved in this stage. It allows members and sub-groups to take leadership in resolving the problem. This process necessitates that members and sub-groups interact and test their strength in relation to others in the group. Often this process may also allow members of the group to test the worker's authority and willingness to distribute some of the power to others.

The essential tasks that members must accomplish in order to move on are related to conflict and its resolution. As members begin to find a place in the group and become more trusting of each other, the worker and the total situation, they are ready to move on to the next group stage. Children, depending on their developmental stage, may accomplish this task to varying degrees. Most children of latency age and older are capable of participating with others in finding their place in a sub-group and/or the group as a whole, but there is more variation in their desire and ability to "wrestle the authority" (Levine, 1979) from the worker so that some of the power is distributed to the members. An instance of this occurred when the worker asked two children if they would like to be in charge of the refreshments at the next session. This allowed the worker to maintain authority and let the children participate by taking on a time-limited responsibility. With older children, who are beginning to work through an identity crisis, there is likely to be much more ability to "struggle" over the distribution of authority in the group and to take and use this power.

These variations in developmental stages can be expected to impact the depth of interactions that occur in the stages that follow. It can be anticipated that generally the younger children will interact with each other in a more shallow way than teenagers might.

In most children's groups, this stage is very difficult and active for the worker, who must remain very alert to communications—both the overt and covert messages being sent. Sometimes, the worker may decide to purposefully not respond. It is only by "passing" the tests of the members and their behavior and allowing the testing of a variety of parameters that the group can work through this phase of development.

In other groups, this stage may be relatively benign and difficult for the worker to differentiate as an identifiable period. The method of working through this stage is dependent on the identified problem, the amount of trust generally held by the members, the sensitivity and skill of the practitioner and perhaps the age of the members. The specific worker behaviors important in helping the group move through this stage are (1) giving support to the development of the group, such as the development of alliances and sub-groups; (2) allowing expression of differences and conflict; and (3) supporting the group members in the resolution of their differences.

The worker encourages a balance between repressive conformity and aggressive "takeover" by members of the group as a whole. The nature of the power, its distribution and uses, must be clarified and experienced by the members during this stage. It is important to create an atmosphere in which this can occur and then support the members and the group in their experimentation with the parameters of power and its use in this setting.

In helping members resolve the issues about inclusion and rejection, the worker actively demonstrates respect and acceptance of all the members and their ideas. The worker models the belief that differences are acceptable or at least can be tolerated.

Throughout this phase of the group, the social worker is able to gain a better understanding of each member and his/her interactions with others, thus producing an assessment with much more depth and breadth. Some of the areas of focus for the worker are: strengthening the relationship between members; continuing the development of values and goals, both of the members and the group as a whole; further clarification of purposes; reduction of resistances that further strengthens the motivation of the members; and, in general, stabilizing the group membership.

This strengthening of relationship and how it occurs is illustrated in one group as follows:

In an ethnically and racially mixed group of eleven- and twelve-year-old girls, Betty was the only white member. She had very low self-esteem and expected rejection from everyone. One of the mechanisms that she used to bolster her esteem was to emphasize her differences from the others. She identified herself with a community reference group and identified the other members in the group with another opposing group. She did this very actively in her style of dress, use of graffiti and other behaviors. She continued in this manner to the point of becoming a scapegoat in the group. Other members had certainly recognized Betty's differences, but now she was flaunting them and forcing some type of confrontation. When this became an issue, the worker talked with Betty, helping her see the part she was playing in others not accepting her. She was able to see that her dress and behavior were much more extreme in the group than it was in school; she consistently went home from school and changed into clothes identified with her reference group before she came to the group sessions.

Betty decided to make some changes in her recent behaviors to gain acceptance by the others. It became clear that this had been accomplished when Betty wet her bed on an overnight trip. The other members were aware of her problem and helped her clean up, thus protecting her from the worker finding out about the situation. (Prior to the trip, the worker had attempted to help Betty and her mother prevent other members from knowing of Betty's enuresis.)

In order for the members to move on to the next stage, they must have moved from nonintimate or parallel relationships to a more intimate system of relationships. As noted previously, there may be a rather wide variation in the depth of accomplishments of this in a children's group because of differences in psychosocial developmental stages. Some amount of balance in power and control must have been attained that allows for autonomy and self-direction. These gains can be expected to result in the enhancement of trust, a commitment to continue in the group and the willingness to be involved at a new level. When these things have occurred, a cohesive unit results. Now there is a *group.*

"Working on My Goals and Those of Other Members"

Stage III. The major characteristic of the members during this span of time, as described by Levine (1979), is that "everyone who is part of the mutual process feels accepted and included in the group, shares in the power and affect of the group, participates in the process of give and take and develops initial empathy" (p. 76). In working with children, the worker must often take the role of helping create empathy between members and of helping members gain and retain power and give-and-take. The children are ready to participate in these ways, but support must be given, sometimes actively, in order to bring out their attitudes and behaviors.

Often, the practitioner models concern and empathy for the member who is experiencing problems or working on a goal. This modeling helps the children make better emotional connections with each other. With latency age children, the worker often acts as a conduit that connects the members with each other. Frequently, the practitioner feels empathy for a child and conveys these emotions to the other children in the group. For example, the worker may notice that a child's behavior is very different from his/her usual functioning. The practitioner may relate this difference to the group and ask why it is happening. This is intended to create an awareness, an interest and an empathy for that member. The worker may then suggest that perhaps one of the children should try to find out what is happening and whether he/she can help. In this instance, the worker must be actively involved, in contrast to a group of older children where one might expect this process to happen spontaneously.

This focus on feelings helps to intensify the involvement and relationships between the members, so that the group's maximum potential for goal achievement can be attained. Certainly, with groups at differing levels of development and ability, the amount of involvement expected may vary greatly.

The major task during this period of time is to deepen the relationships between members and to work on their therapeutic goals. With the further differentiation of each child that occurs during this process, members broaden their perspective of problem situations and problem-solving behaviors and are more able to use differences as a resource for working on their own goals.

The psychosocial development of the members will be a very important factor in determining their level of ability to make maximal use of the group process for goal accomplishment. When they are only able to function at a very surface level, the worker can help provide more depth in the manner described previously. As individuation occurs and differences in the group become clearer, members can either perceive this as a threat to themselves or see it as a way to expand their boundaries of knowledge, understanding and parameters of their own behavioral repertoire.

It is often the practitioner who is instrumental in helping members see a difference in thinking and/or behavior as a resource for the other members.

Tom was very aggressive and hostile when he came to the group session. After some acting out, he was able to calm down enough to tell the group that he had just received his grades and had failed English. He did not think that this was the grade he deserved and had asked the teacher, "Why did you give me that grade?" She responded, "Because you deserved it!" Tom had really wanted to understand how his grade had been determined but had not received that answer, only a curt reply. The worker recognized that the tone of voice and manner in which Tom had asked the question had no doubt influenced the response that he received.

The other group members became engaged in problem-solving about how Tom still might be able to find the answer to his question. Lenny, who was somewhat withdrawn and not as accepted as some of the other boys, suggested that Tom could ask the teacher, "Could you explain why I received this grade?" After some discussion by others regarding ways to ask the teacher, the members role-played the different possibilities. Tom and the other members were able to decide that Lenny's suggested method was going to be the most helpful in gaining the desired information.

During this third stage, "Empathy provides the haven, sustenance, and energy for members to grow in the group" (Levine, 1979, p. 201). Members can be expected to be accepting and anxious to be helpful. They are able to share feelings and understand those of others. Power is shared among the members, with some guidance from the worker for the younger children. There are often differences of opinion, and conflicts may be frequent but now relatively easy to resolve.

As this group stage develops, there may be areas of gratification for members (Levine, 1979, pp. 206–213). In the beginning, members become aware and begin to utilize their newfound interdependency. Another source of gratification is in the area of relationship issues. Intimacy, the increase in give-and-take and the lack of factionalism (through subgroups) all enhance the members' pleasure in participation.

"We Prepare Ourselves and End the Group"

Stage IV. This stage involving endings and separation of the members is very much a part of the therapeutic process. This is a period of culmination when it is hoped that the gains of members are stabilized and integrated into their total thinking and behavior as a frame of reference and are available for use with others outside the group.

The primary issues to be worked on during this stage are separation and evaluation of the group experience and the progress of each member. This often is a time of real ambivalence for the members. Separation may be a very emotional process, as the children are losing the worker and also many friends that they have made. This pain may be greater for some because of the recollection of other unresolved separations in the past. It may also be a time of gratification and satisfaction for the children because of the progress and gains they have made.

As the members become more aware of the imminence of ending, they mobilize their defenses. This often takes the form of moving apart, insulating themselves, lessening their empathy and making connections with others outside the group. Initially, there may be denial and regression. The members may pretend not to hear the worker's talk about ending, by not responding or continuing to plan for future group activities as if nothing was going to happen. This occurred in one group as follows:

One worker began to question herself. Had she indeed told the group on a number of occasions that it was soon time for the group to end? Why did the members not care enough to talk about it? Then the worker overheard a nonmember ask one of the members about joining the group. The member responded that the group would be ending soon. She and the others had heard the worker's message but were not yet ready to deal with it. This member's comments about the reality of endings now opened the subject to discussion by the group.

Nostalgia may occur spontaneously, providing for recapitulation that may include both reenactment and review of previous situations and members' behaviors.

During a weekend outing in a cabin in the mountains, a group of boys (who were beginning the termination process) sat together and talked about the many roles the worker had played. They said, ''he's like my father''; ''he's a big brother to me''; ''he was a teacher for me''; and ''sometimes he was like a probation officer.''

The group may also become involved in the mourning process: feeling depressed, hostile, guilty and fearful. They may feel abandoned by the worker and join together in being angry at and attacking him/her. This may be enacted by either overt or covert behavior. Some may ''flee'' from the group and not return after it becomes evident that, in fact, the group is ending.

Once some of these feelings about endings and termination have been worked through, members are often more able to focus on the accomplishments that they have made. If goals have been identified, others can give positive feedback about even small gains that each member has made throughout the life of the group. Often special celebrations, activities or parties are used for the final session of the group. This provides an opportunity for further reinforcement regarding the gains made by giving a special note to each child or some other item that confirms his/her success and achievements.

An essential concern of the practitioner during this time is to help members work through their feelings and leave the group without a sense of abandonment. Focusing on the successes of members can help support their competencies in coping and increase their confidence in their ability to function successfully.

The social worker helps members to (1) deal with their denial and other negative feelings; (2) evaluate progress; (3) stabilize gains; and (4) develop bonds with others outside the group. During the life of the group, "the members have found mutual acceptance and respect and have participated actively in a process of mutual aid. Now termination of a member or the breaking up of a group needs to be done in such a way that ending becomes a dynamic growth-producing experience" (Northen, 1988, p. 298).

SUMMARY

With this overview of group stages, it is possible to now cover the other major area of knowledge required to begin to plan a group—the developmental stages of the child. This is explicated in the following chapter.

Chapter 2

The Latency Age Child

Along with the stages of group development, it is essential to keep in mind the developmental stages of the children who are being considered for membership. Knowledge about and immediate awareness of this material is crucial to thinking about and planning when forming a group for therapeutic purposes.

As the practitioner plans a group of children, it is essential to think about what would a group of seven- and eight-year-old boys, or nine-year-old girls be like? How could they be expected to behave? What would their interests be? What are the developmental tasks that must be accomplished at there ages? Obviously, the answers can not be very precise until the worker has gathered information and at least interviewed the likely members, but a broad picture of the potential group can be brought to mind to assist the worker in the planning stage and in assessing the possible members.

TRANSITION TO MIDDLE YEARS

In order to understand the latency period, often referred to as middle childhood, it is important to be aware of the tasks and issues that are of concern to children in the previous stage, early childhood. Preschool children must deal with separation and individuation issues. In most instances, trust has been learned in the home, and now it is necessary to transfer that trust to relationships outside the home, primarily in the school setting. During this adjustment to the new setting, children are often learning and practicing new roles with peers. Their development is increasingly influenced by new ideas and contact with a variety of roles, such as those of school teachers, acquaintances and neighbors. They also find themselves in circumstances in which they must adapt and cope.

As the child enters school, many changes in development are occurring. By the age of five or six years, as noted by Sarnoff (1980), "the child can project his feelings of love and jealousy, rage and destruction, into fantasy with such skill that he frightens himself" (p. 151). It is during the latency period that integration of these feelings and ways of expressing them are worked through. Especially in early childhood and the beginning of the latency period, "play is the great laboratory for the child's integrative experiments" (Sarnoff, 1987, p. 220).

It is generally believed that children before the age of seven years are not sufficiently oriented to peers to make effective use of groups (Garland & West, 1984). Groups of pre-latency children may be useful in socializing but are not useful in providing any depth of treatment or helping the children make major changes. Basically, children of this age are egocentric. Even though several children are playing together in a room, each child is in essence playing by him/herself with other children present; that is, they are all involved in parallel play.

DYNAMICS OF THE LATENCY STAGE

Sigmund Freud and his followers had viewed this period of child development as a quiescent, dormant, latent time. As more study and understanding of this stage of life has been accomplished, this has been referred to as a "myth of quiescence." It is now well known and accepted that latency is a stage in which change occurs in almost all areas of the child's life. There is often disagreement about when this stage of development begins and ends. Williams (1972) proposed a division of this broader period into three specific stages: early latency from five to seven years, latency proper from seven to nine years and late latency from nine to eleven years. These groupings have not generally been accepted, because it is viewed as misleading to use such arbitrary divisions.

In fact, the actual timing of the beginning and ending of this period of development is difficult to determine and may differ from child to child. It is influenced by at least three factors: behavioral expectations of the environment, normal maturational unfolding, and the capacity to enter into a state of latency (Sarnoff, 1980). This is a part of the assessment of each child that must be made by the social worker in composing the group, so that there will be commonality in the level of development of the members.

This school-age period is the beginning of the end of the child's egocentric outlook and the start of a true social orientation. Schechter and Combrink-Graham (1991) describe the expected outcomes to be derived. "The child in the middle years has developed a personal competence in language, motor, and ego functioning which allows him to present himself to society like a butterfly emerging from the chrysalis—sticky, shaky, unpracticed but equipped to try himself in a larger world—to be introduced, as Erikson put it, to the 'technology of this society' (p. 299)." During this stage, there are three major thrusts in the child's life: an increased facility in physical and neurophysiological skills, a move away from the influence of home and toward greater peer influence and the child's growing ability to think, conceptualize and use symbolism (Cohen, 1972).

During these middle childhood years, children are attempting to deal with an active exchange between their inner world and the world around them. "Thus, in the period of latency, two opposing processes are set in motion. At first there is an incorporation and formalization of parental social attitudes, making possible the continuity of culture. Social flexibility, in the form of opening of the mind to social forces at odds with the family ethics, becomes available in late latency" (Sarnoff, 1980, p. 148). Anna Freud (1965, p. 32) describes this major task to be accomplished as follows: "The ego of the young child has the developmental task to master on the one hand orientation in the external world and on the other hand the chaotic emotional states which exist within himself." Integration becomes a procedure used by the child in an attempt to resolve these conflicting processes. By using this means, the child attempts to create a balance, an equilibrium where various aspects, such as action, play, dreaming and introspection, all can find their place within the structure of self (Berger, 1974).

A Psychological State

"Actually, the state of latency (calm, pliability, and educability) is the result of an active process of organization of ego functions in the service of social demands" (Sarnoff, 1987, p. 5). This state of good behavior is maintained as a result of an ever-changing equilibrium between the drives and defenses of the child. When drives are activated, the child uses a series of defenses to directly control their expression. Fantasy is one of the ways in which the drives are controlled. The fantasies are then actively reorganized and synthesized into highly symbolized, displaced stories. By living through these stories in play, the child finds safety valves for the drives that are experienced (Sarnoff, 1987).

Some of the defenses available to the child at this age are sublimation, obsessive-compulsive activities, doing and undoing, reaction formation and repression. They are used by the child to adapt to a world that requires social compliance and ability to acquire knowledge. More specifically, the steps involved in the child's working through the control of a drive may be as follows. First, after a typical preoccupation or forbidden wish has been defended against, it becomes unconscious and is referred to as a latent fantasy. These fantasies are then worked through by using daydreams, fantasy and play (Ohrenstein, 1986). They discharge the drives and protect the mental equilibrium of the latency stage. This is a way of dealing with conflict in thought rather than in reality. The patterns of defense secured during this stage will influence the expression of drives during adolescence.

The experiences of the child stir up preoccupations, questions and thoughts that may be very engrossing. One way of dealing with this is to regress to an earlier stage, which may involve messing and smearing as a method for dealing with anger. Another commonly used defense to deal with rage is reaction formation, which produces calmness, cleanliness and good behavior and may be accompanied by obsessive behavior such as collecting almost anything, like baseball cards, bottle caps or string. Even when this form of defense is used, there may still be frequent periods of regression to the messing stage.

In addition to the usual defensive measures, the child carefully monitors acceptable behavioral patterns (i.e., athletics, school recess and physical education classes) and uses them as a primary outlet for aggression. This focus on environment and social situations is essential to the child's development of a self-concept and identification through object relationships.

When there is a readiness, the child gathers and uses information about expected behavioral patterns. This data is integrated and retained by the child, becoming a part of the ego ideal. At the same time, the child channels energies into places and situations where more direct discharge of drives is acceptable (Sarnoff, 1987).

Even though there are problems in dividing the latency period into sub-stages, because of the number of years involved in this phase, it is useful to identify at least two major time periods. Sarnoff (1987) identifies one as the early phase, the six- to eight-year-old period, and the other as the later phase, the eight- to twelve-year-old period.

During the early phase, children are preoccupied with themselves. The child is frequently described as "being too big for his boots." Individual energy is used to improve self and for the conquest of people and things (Maier, 1969). In this early stage, fantasies contain amorphous monsters and are used as a defense. Children at age seven or eight begin to feel a sense of independence from parents and are confronted with fear as they realize how small, vulnerable and alone they are in the big world. This is often reflected in the fear of monsters that masks the representations of real fears. Reality is only used by the child to "disengage himself from untenable and unfulfillable drives and fantasies" (Sarnoff, 1987, p. 33).

At about the age of nine, children shift from focusing mental and emotional energies on parents as a primary arbiter of social behavior. They now place more attention on the environment and the social situation in which they live. During this time, the outside world becomes increasingly more available as a source of objects through which fantasies can be gratified. The fantasies contain figures that resemble real people. The earlier fantasized monsters now become witches and robbers. In late latency, the fantasies are no longer used but are replaced with real situations and real objects.

Earlier in latency, fantasies are used for problem-solving; conflicts are played out through thought, rather than in reality. Now, in later latency, there is a gradual shift to the use of more reality-oriented defenses. Some tactics used in late latency to master overwhelming stress include doing to another what has been done to oneself, talking about an experience directly or developing a fantasy to overcome the circumstances. This latter tactic may involve creating a comforting inner-world fantasy in which the child is the powerful baseball player, the most popular girl in the school or a famous movie star (Sarnoff, 1987). "Latency-age children rarely request help for themselves. It is difficult for them to express their unhappiness in words, and they are likely to express their problems through behavior" (Lieberman, 1979, pp. 133–134).

During these middle years, not only are aggressive drives expressed in fantasy and play but in competitiveness, self-blame, self-doubt and self-injury. The aggression in these instances is turned inward.

A major task for mastery during middle childhood is a realization of competence. This is accomplished as described by Erikson as a sense of industry versus a sense of inferiority. During this stage, there are pulls in two opposing directions. One side puts unceasing energy into efforts to produce, the other side pulls toward a previous level of less production (Maier, 1969). Acquisition of skills and accomplishments in school (a sense of industry) is critical to feelings of well-being, pride and self-esteem. Doing well in school leads to feelings of personal power. This is a very vulnerable period of time as lack of task accomplishment may lead to interference with identity development. Feelings of competency are exceedingly important during this time. If children do not believe that they measure up to peers, they may feel shame because of physical defects, exposure of failures and loss of control. Feelings of inferiority are frequently coupled with shame.

As mastery of the basic tasks of this stage is achieved—control of impulses and adaptation to the real world—the source of self-esteem becomes more integrated. The self acts as a selective filter for development of areas of competence and acceptance and thus self-esteem. After this has occurred, the child is less vulnerable to minor slights, and the impact of praise on self-esteem depends largely on the value to the child of what is being praised and by whom (Garbarino, Stott et al., 1992). Now, real ability can regulate the self-esteem and contribute to a sense of self and identity.

When children are constantly unable to master challenges, they may experience lowered self-esteem, depression, anxiety and other pathological symptoms. Self-esteem may also be lowered when the child compares him/herself unfavorably to a dissonant reference group, such as a black child attending a primarily white school. Rosenberg (1979) found that it is primarily contextual dissonance that damages self-esteem rather than one's ethnic or religious identification per se. "The acquisition of self-concepts and identifications through internalization of experiences with objects in the environment are pertinent to the future of the child in society" (Sarnoff, 1987, p. 12).

By approximately nine years of age, children have begun a process of psychological separation from their parents. With the development in all areas that has occurred to this time, the parents are now seen as more human and fallible. Children are likely to become more critical of their perceived shortcomings. There is much ambivalence and movement backward and forward in this rejection of parents. This is the time when children may wonder if they "are really adopted," whether these are their "real parents," or why are their parents not perfect? This prepuberty stage follows them into the adolescent phase where even more separation from parents can be expected to become evident (Lieberman, 1979).

The meaning of psychological development for the worker. By understanding the psychological development of children during this phase of development, the social worker is prepared to work with a variety of behaviors from a child. As is evident, one may also expect that there will be rapid shifts from one type of activity to another as the child shifts between the pulls of "industry versus inferiority." For example, a child has a desire to be productive and to produce a present for Mother's Day. Feeling unsuccessful, he/she may throw the object in the air, destroy it and then feel depressed and worthless. These feelings may persist and cause him/her to want others to be unsuccessful too, leading to acting out and attempts to destroy others' craft work.

The child can be expected to be open to learning about the world through a broad array of experiences. Not only does the child learn from experiencing each incident him/herself, in a group there are opportunities to learn by observing others and their interactions with people and objects in society.

Not only are experiences important in middle childhood, it is also important that each child in the group experience the feelings associated with being successful. It is essential that the social worker plan activities or programs that focus on individual children and the opportunities for them to be successful within that activity. Sometimes, it is even important to plan the role that will be assigned to a particular child, allowing him/her to experience success. An example of this planning is asking a girl who is moving toward the scapegoat role to be in charge of serving refreshments at the next session, a highly prized role in her group. The worker is then aware of any opportunity to praise her and her performance in this task. Obviously, the praise must be real and honest, and mistakes on the girl's part ignored by plan.

An activity that can be very important for children of this age would be one that allows room for fantasy. It might involve anything from miming a song, to acting out a skit, to going to a park and swinging on a rope on a large tree. This allows for some skill development but also may promote fantasies for children that they may use differently to meet their own needs.

Physical Growth

During the latency years, growth generally tends to be slow and relatively constant. Maier (1969) notes that "physical maturation slows as if to consolidate what has already been acquired" (p. 54). Some children, however, may have growth spurts between the ages of six and eight years. Growth that is rather significant in this stage is hand-eye coordination and fine muscle coordination, which generally develops about the age of eight years. As a result of this changing capacity, new skill development is possible.

Even though there is slow, steady growth throughout this stage, "The latency-age child is physically too small to express his aggressive drives effectively in his relationship with adult caretakers" (Lieberman, 1979, p. 6). Even by the time of prepuberty, the child still depends on adult control but to a lesser degree.

The most important area for concentration for latency age children is their capacity to relate and communicate with the most significant individuals in their life—peers. Children strive toward being the best, strongest, fastest and wittiest. They ward off failure at almost any price.

Generally at about the age of eleven or twelve, there is an increase in secretion of hormones and a beginning change in attitudes, behavior and ways of relating among peers.

Physical growth and its significance in group composition. In summary, there is a very wide range of physical change within this developmental stage, and if the child is lagging in maturation he/she may be quite different from peers of the same age. For example, six-year-olds seem to be in constant motion. They enjoy physical activity, such as jumping, wrestling, playing tag and tumbling with other children, but their movements may be clumsy because of fatigue (Kohlberg, 1969). Seven-year-olds, in contrast, are less active than six-year-olds. Their posture is more tense and ready for motion, and they enjoy skating and active sports. At the same time, they enjoy opportunities to sit down and rest. Certainly, one can expect that some seven-year-olds are lagging in developmental maturation, because there is a mix of behaviors in any group of the same age.

By the age of nine, there is even more variation in skills. There is much more skill in manual activities and an ability to use both hands independently. Often children desire perfection, and they move toward development of more refined muscular control and ability to manipulate objects.

Based on the physical descriptions of possible latency age members, it may be very important to carefully assess the physical maturation and skill development of potential members before forming a group.

Cognitive Development

The latency period is a turning point with its development of concrete operational thinking. During this period of growth, abstractions can now be appreciated and applied to concrete situations. This makes the use of fantasy less useful for the discharge of drives. "Magical fulfillment through fantasy succumbs to reality" (Sarnoff, 1987, p. 11).

Entrance into school is symbolic of the crucial issues of the latency period. Children learn that tasks and problems have solutions, and they need to engage in cognitive activity to solve them. As children move through this stage to early adolescence, their thinking abilities are much more like those of the adult (Flavell, 1985). Children are increasingly able to coordinate information from differing perspectives and points of view. They are able to go beyond immediate appearances to make logical inferences based on reasoning.

During these middle years, children develop an increasing awareness of their own thought processes. As this happens, they develop an increasing ability to reflect on and direct their own cognitive behaviors. They become more aware of what they know and what they do not know.

Not only do children develop more abstract thinking skills, they also increasingly refine verbalization and language skills. They acquire a fascination with jokes, foreign words and phrases, secret codes and languages such as Pig Latin.

As their abilities to reason and verbalize grow, children often challenge the ideas and beliefs of adults. This frequently leads to modification and changes of the beliefs of the children as they gain experience and relationships in a variety of settings.

In terms of morality, Piaget (1952) has pointed out that "the latency age child moves from morality of restraint to the morality of cooperation; from rigid standards about punishment to one where motivation and social implication of an act is appreciated and greatly affects the parent-child relationship" (p. 148). Children of this age may oppose and question the motivation of adults in setting rules and enforcing them. They now want to share in the power that the adult has possessed up to this point and share in the decision-making process. They not only want to participate, they may demand their rights and fairness of treatment for others as well.

The memory of the child is changing in significant ways during this stage of development. This allows for an increasing fund of knowledge and experiences. In early latency, the reliability of memory may be questionable. As indicated in a study by Saywitz (1987), younger children were more vulnerable to various kinds of suggestions. He found that eight- and nine-year-olds tended "to remember less and embellish more" (Saywitz, 1987, p. 48). In contrast, by the age of eleven or twelve, the memory ability was as complete as that of an adult. Memory has a great effect on learning ability. Flavell (1985) noted, "What the head knows has an enormous effect on what the head learns and remembers" (p. 213).

For pre-latency children, their values are absolute—a thing is either all good or all bad. By the age of seven, they begin to view events from more than one perspective and become less rigid in the area of cognitive development. At the same time, the reasoning ability of the seven-year-old is still limited to concrete situations, not to abstractions. Older children begin to order their experiences. At approximately seven and a half or eight years of age, the child develops an ability to remember abstract aspects of experiences, which then can be recalled and used. This new ability may be expressed in a variety of ways, such as through the motor level (modeling clay), verbal level (verbal descriptions), or abstract level (use of metaphors, poems, etc.) (Sarnoff, 1987).

In later latency, children acquire the capacity to perform reversibility, which is "the permanent possibility of returning to the starting point of the operation in question" (Inhelder & Piaget, 1958, p. 272). Now children are able to explore a variety of possible solutions to a problem, not adopt any of them and return to their original position. They are aware of many approaches to one situation.

The perception and behaviors related to rules change during middle childhood. At the age of seven and eight, children have a very rigid respect for rules, even though they may argue about them. Toward the end of the middle years, the child begins to understand the "spirit" of the law rather than the "letter."

Six- and seven-year-olds are still in the pre-operative stage and not sensitive to intentions and feeling of others. Over time, children develop a range of skills and strategies such as planning, predicting, checking, monitoring, testing, reviewing, revising, rehearsing and categorizing (Garbarino, Stott et al., 1992). The capacity to reason affects their awareness and understanding of the difference between fantasy and reality, and truth and lies. As children mature, they are able to make finer distinctions in rules, norms and values. There is a disconnection of thought from objects and a liberation of relations.

In general, children from nine to twelve years of age are interested in rules that will regulate their mutual activities. They strive toward objectivity in enforcement and expect equity in punishment. For them, violation of reciprocity is an extremely serious crime, and lies are defined objectively. By late latency, children have a better grasp of motivational factors and a beginning idea of subjective responsibility. (Previously their judgment had been based on consequences of their behaviors.)

The meaning of cognitive development for the practitioner. As is evident from the previous discussion, working with the latency age child can be viewed as a real challenge. Because of the many facets of the cognitive area and the possible range of development in any group, it is impossible to readily assess where a child is in relation to any one specific aspect. This is significant, because the worker needs to plan program so that the child with the greatest deficit can still participate in the activity. Usually, this can only be determined as children begin to take part in a planned activity, and as the practitioner observes behavior. Sometimes, it is important for the worker to alter or modify some part of the activity or to change it entirely in order to allow everyone to participate.

Some differences may be viewed as healthy and growth-producing if the disparity is not too great between individuals in the group. Variation in the children's perception of rules, ability to remember and to view differing perspectives, morality and varying degrees of verbal refinement may not impede interaction between the children. Even the use of fantasy by the early latency child may provide a welcome relief from the greater degree of reality thinking of the more mature child. Differences in reasoning ability of members (concrete thinking versus abstract thinking) would seem to create the most incompatibility and rejection of some children by others and cause the most problems in planning activities in which everyone could participate.

Sexual Development

For latency age children, sexual interest continues but may not be of primary focus. Sexuality at this age is expressed most often through movement of the whole body in play activity. During this stage of development, activities are limited to children of the same sex. Children of the opposite sex are generally kept at a distance and sometimes despised or teased. It is during this time that "the group tends to encourage and reward members who master the stereotyped sexual roles of class and culture" (Lieberman, 1979, p. 81).

Application of knowledge regarding sexual development. Groups of latency age children should always be composed of either all boys or all girls, unless there is some specific identifiable purpose for mixing them in one group. Short-term groups, because they are focused on a very specific purpose and often are related to a crisis such as divorce, death or bereavement, are the exception to the rule.

Social Development

It is during these middle childhood years when a sense of belonging is developed. It seems that the peer group takes on a greater importance even than that of the family. This lays a foundation for identification with the community and country.

Socialization of the child now expands beyond the immediate environment of the home. There is opportunity to remedy eccentricities of values and cultural idiosyncrasies that have been picked up during childhood socialization (Sullivan, 1953).

No longer does the child appear to be motivated by self-interest but rather by shared interest with a group where more give-and-take occurs. During this time, children often involve themselves with creative play that has no preestablished rules, thus allowing for collective agreement to occur. This is a time of gaining acceptance and becoming an integral part of the peer group and later the society. "Both sexes show interest in organizing clubs; these serve to increase the distance from the family and also strengthen the nonparental superego" (Kramer & Rudolph, 1991, p. 324).

During this time, the child can use "passive identification with myths and legends provided by the child's social group" (Sarnoff, 1987, p. 7). Through these experiences, children acquire cultural patterns of behavior, rituals and beliefs that will guide their life, opinions, mores and social reactions for a lifetime. Once a socially approved doctrine of behavior is internalized and becomes identified with the individual, children will reject new inputs as foreign.

As children mature, they learn to evaluate others and themselves. On entering school, they develop and expand their understanding of authority. Now they recognize the policeman, the crossing guard and perhaps even the teacher as forms of authority. This assists them in learning ways of evaluating peers and peer behavior. Observing how peers are treated by authority figures helps children begin to measure their own behavior.

At first, children have little sensitivity to the feelings of others; this results in a rigid, cruel society. As time goes by, the pressures of society force them to give up many of the ideas of childhood. By the age of nine or ten, the children are able to put themselves into the shoes of another (Minuchin, 1977). Empathy, compassion and acceptance of self and others, regardless of differences that may be observed, are possible outcomes of group participation.

In the middle years, children actively develop mastery and independence in their relationships. Customs are transmitted from class to class. Sayings such as "Step on a crack, break your mother's back" fit well with the obsessive-compulsive defenses used during this period of life.

Peers and play are all important. Peers become the "experts," and conforming to peer standards is exceedingly important. A girl's best friend is an exaggerated friendship; it's almost a love affair. Boys, too, develop best friends. Their relationships usually exclude girls and parents, and they are inclined to seek out adults in science, shop or physical education (Lieberman, 1979).

Loyalty to the group becomes very important. Interest in the body is handled through jokes, secrets and whispering, and there are new concerns with grooming. Generally during this time the children are becoming more flexible in their attitudes and are concerned about their school and neighborhood.

In relation to parents and family, preschool children have been involved in sibling rivalry and continue this relationship throughout the middle years. They participate in games that allow them to win in reality rather than in fantasy. By the age of nine or ten, children often begin to object to parental interference. They want to run their own lives and may begin to defy parents by saying, "Don't treat me like a baby!"

Use of knowledge about social development in the group. "Normalcy" for the latency age child involves behaviors that may alternate between two polarities. One end of the continuum is represented in behaviors manifested in intermittent periods of excitement and drive activity; the other pole is represented by alternating periods of calm. The notion of pathology is often identified as an exaggeration of periods of time at either polarity (inappropriate calm or inappropriate excitement).

There may be a skewed form of development for children from lower socioeconomic subcultures, which makes it discordant with the dominant society (Sarnoff, 1987). Since progress during latency is shaped by the environment and parenting, for some children there may be permanent interference with accomplishments expected to lead to success as determined by society. For example, if the child during latency is impacted with a continual high level of excitement, this would be detrimental to the calm pursuit of goals and the ordering and reordering necessary for successfully moving through this developmental stage. "By definition, children who fail to enter latency have difficulty in achieving self-control through self-quieting activities" (Sarnoff, 1987, p. 81).

If the child does not move through the latency stage, several negative consequences can be expected in later life. There may be an inability to develop future plans based on reality, poor organizational skills and sense of time and an inability to cope effectively with problems and humiliations.

To facilitate the child in moving successfully through this stage, activities and experiences in the group are exceedingly important. As noted by Northen (1988), there is a close interrelationship between facility in verbalization and exposure to, and use of, experiences in the social and physical environment. The lack of language skills that may result from this deficit in experiences may be reflected in poor performance in school and work.

With the information provided in Chapters 1 and 2 on group theory and development during the middle childhood years, it is time to consider the planning and recruitment of children for the group, which is discussed in Chapter 3.

PART II

DEVELOPMENT AND USE OF
THE GROUP

Chapter 3

Planning for the Group

With an awareness and understanding of both group and individual stages of development, the practitioner is ready to begin the process of planning, which is essential for forming and recruiting a group of children. Decisions must be made about a variety of factors in order to produce positive outcomes. Simply participating in a group does not necessarily produce these desired results. The worker's planning and ongoing participation and guidance are essential to success.

Group participation and outcomes may be experienced by members, the worker and others as either positive or negative. The meaning and value of the group is determined by a variety of complex forces. The factors that are believed to contribute to effective group services cannot be left to chance but must be carefully thought through and planned. As noted by Kurland (1978, p. 173), "The price for lack of thorough and thoughtful planning is high. Frequently, it is paid in groups that terminate prematurely, groups in which attendance of members is sporadic and irregular, and groups that are felt by practitioners and group members to have failed in meeting the needs of group members."

The first decision to be made by an agency or organization is whether group services should be provided and, if so, for what populations or types of problems or needs. The stimulation to consider providing group services may come from a variety of sources. Most often, the notion of providing group services comes from the administrator(s) of an agency, the social worker or the clients themselves. Sometimes these services have been requested by others in the community, such as the vice-principal in a local school, the parent of a child in the neighborhood or a local businessperson who has observed some of the children with problem behaviors in his/her establishment.

Groups established by an agency often have purposes directly related to its goals as described in an overall program narrative (Garvin, 1981). The purpose for founding a settlement house, for example, was to serve the community living around that establishment: to act as a "neighbor to the neighbors," assisting them in whatever ways possible. It came to the attention of the administrators that many of the children were being left alone after school, with no one to care for or supervise them. This was a community with a great deal of gang activity, primarily involving older adolescents and young adults. Agency personnel decided that several after-school clubs should be established to meet the needs of the younger children. The agency's purpose is broad—to serve the community living around the institution—while the purposes of the groups are much narrower and more specific—to help the children develop more positive peer relationships and to have fun. Even though these purposes are stated at differing levels of abstraction, they are in accord with each other. The purpose of the children's groups can thus be included along with many others under the goals of the agency.

If the decision to have groups is made by an agency's administrative board, the social work employees in that setting have the responsibility to consider the various purposes that can be accomplished through the use of groups. At the same time, the administrators need to be aware that they may support certain purposes that are inappropriate for the groups. For example, a number of people on the program committee wanted to use the groups to get a specific ethnic group to dress and look more like the majority of people in society. The reason for setting this goal was a belief that if the ethnic groups did not look so different from one another, the conflict between them would not be so overt. The underlying intent of helping the groups get along better was commendable, but the proposed method for doing this was not acceptable to the social worker as a professional.

If the agency traditionally has not conducted a group program, ideally, it would first develop a plan that may involve administrative details such as: providing meeting rooms of the size and quality needed for the proposed activities, selecting or hiring a worker(s) and buying new furnishings and/or supplies. Often, the reality of the situation is that the worker attempts to modify and alter already existing rooms to be used for meetings and finds potential materials for activities whenever possible.

Another common way for groups to be established is when a worker(s) recognizes that the agency is seeing more and more individuals with similar problems or needs. After becoming aware of this commonality of problems, the worker may decide that a group is the most effective way of helping these clients. This recognition of common client needs may either come from the caseload of one worker or from several workers' discussions about problems affecting many agency clients, such as problems with school or family, peer relationships, or separation and divorce of parents. Sometimes the decision to form a group may simply come from a staff member's observations that children are being negatively affected by a common occurrence in that community, such as experiencing a shooting or other form of violence, or the death of a significant other. It may be a staff member who recognizes that children are not being supervised after school and that services are needed.

Sometimes groups are established after referrals are made by someone in the community. Most often, this seems to be the principal or vice-principal at school. These referrals may be a list of individuals who are having difficulty or a group of children who are often involved together in troublesome behavior (a natural group). Another source of referrals may be professionals in other agencies who recognize the children's need for services but do not have the resources to meet those needs themselves. A few referrals may be made by businesspersons in the neighborhood or by the police, who have identified children getting into trouble in the community.

Sometimes, these referrals are made rather formally; at other times, the need for services may be presented in a rather direct, yet informal, manner as indicated in the following example:

One of the male social workers, in an agency that works with delinquent and predelinquent children, did not have a group one afternoon and was doing paperwork in a very quiet office. Suddenly, there was a great commotion in another room of the building. He hurried to the room to see what was happening and found three young boys being chased by a policeman. The boys had been shoplifting and had run into the building to get away from "the law." As a result, they had actively referred themselves for services by this agency. When seeing the boys' dilemma, the worker offered them services, which they readily accepted as the police officer waited for their answer.

In some agencies, parents can be a frequent source of referrals. They may recognize that their child is having some difficulty and may actively seek assistance with the problem.

In a few cases, a final source of referrals may be the children themselves. Sometimes, a child who has participated in a group may refer another child to that organization. In some cases, the child may be able to state what he/she gained from the group experience and to recognize that others could be helped by similar experiences.

Regardless of the source that leads to forming a group, it is not uncommon for the agency administrators to request that a description of the group, its purpose and a plan for services be submitted for approval before moving on to form and organize a group. In order to accomplish this task, other planning must be done and decisions made. If the agency is just beginning a group work program for children, for example, there may be inconveniences that may result, such as noisier halls, greater risk of property damage, additional clerical and staff time, some difficulty controlling the children and the need to purchase special supplies (Siepker & Kandaras, 1985). Consideration of these issues must also be a part of the decision-making process for the organizational personnel.

PURPOSE

All of the methods just described may bring children to a particular agency for service. However, before planning can proceed, it is important to carefully assess specific problems and needs of the child or the group that is being considered. A primary concern is whether these problems or needs and the manner in which they may be manifested can be tolerated and included within the agency's conceptualization of purpose and the physical structure and environment of the agency. After a broad group purpose is determined, for example, "to help children of divorce cope with their new situations and their resulting feelings," individual goals may be set.

Individual goals may include any of the following of numerous possibilities. Jay's goal may be to reestablish a relationship with his father; Mary's goal is to learn to be alone in the home after school until her mother returns from work; Tom needs to improve his grades in school, which have dropped dramatically since his father moved from the family home. All of these children's goals are the outcome of the new situation in their lives created by the divorce of their parents. The children's goals stated here are long-term goals, goals that are expected to be accomplished by the end of the group. Each of the long-term goals will need to be implemented with the planning and utilization of more immediate interim goals as the group progresses.

This broad statement of group purpose is deliberately stated in a general and global manner so that it encompasses a variety of individual problems and needs. At a later time, members will be able to respond to it and to modify or change it to fit their particular needs and desires, so that the group really becomes their group. (This will be discussed further in a later chapter.)

OTHER GROUP DIMENSIONS TO BE PLANNED

Purpose is the primary factor around which all planning revolves. It is only as this major objective is decided that decisions about group size, duration, composition and other planning dimensions can be resolved.

If the purpose of the group is very focused and specific, a short-term group of six to eight weeks may be formed. For example, a group for children of divorce, if carefully planned and developed, may be appropriate for a short-term group. Other purposes, such as helping children get along better in school, may require a much longer duration in order to meet the variety of goals of most children.

Group Size

There is general agreement that small groups for therapeutic purposes should have a maximum of eight or nine members. In children's groups, depending on the number of workers and the age and problems of the children, there is some agreement that a maximum of seven children may be the optimum size. If only one practitioner is involved, a group of five or six members may be most advantageous. Often, the number of members is finally determined by the developmental level of the children and their mode of expressing their concerns as well as the level of experience of the worker.

Especially with young children, seven and eight years old, two workers may be most desirable to help with any activities that require assistance or to deal with a crisis that may occur in the session. If one child must leave the group for any reason, a single worker often finds him/ herself in a dilemma, trying to decide which is the most crucial situation—the individual child or the others in the group.

Another factor to consider in determining the size of the group is the manner in which the communication patterns of members may be affected. With early latency age children, it is predictable that the major source of communication, both verbal and nonverbal, will be the worker(s). The child at this age is still very centered on the adult(s) in the situation. Developmental lags that may have occurred could make this even more pronounced (see Chapter 2). A small group may thus be very desirable for this type of client.

In contrast, older latency children have sometimes been identified as being the gang age, a time when peers become very important. Garbarino, Stott et al. (1992, p. 33) describe this period as a time when "their allegiance to peers is now often a powerful motivating force for sharing or refusing to share information." A larger group may be preferred for the older child.

The worker must remember that if the group is very small, member-to-member interaction certainly will be intensified. This is in comparison to a group of seven to nine children, where the size may promote early development of sub-groups. This may or may not be desirable, since sub-groups may influence the group in either positive or negative ways. Early development of these groups will require the worker to focus on another factor in the total relationships and communication among members.

There are other factors related to group size that must be considered in planning a group. With young latency age children, a group that is "too large" may provide a situation that overstimulates and creates confusion for the members. They may need small groups to allow them a safe place to move toward mastery of themselves and of situations. It must be noted that there are also some cultural differences in the degree of readiness for group participation that must be taken in account. In addition, Northen (1988, p. 130) says that "children from large, economically deprived families are often not yet ready for the intimacy of a small group."

Another reason for using small groups is that generally children are unlikely to postpone attention to themselves and their concerns for any length of time (Garvin, 1981, pp. 79–80). Children who can be expected to be aggressive and destructive also will require rather small groups, since the worker will need to deal with an individual's behavior and the rest of the group at the same time.

Obviously, there are not clear-cut rules regarding the appropriate size for a particular group. The decisions to be made about group size must be based on the judgment of the person(s) doing the planning, using as much of the knowledge and practice wisdom as is available.

Duration

Duration is another factor that is important to consider in planning a group. The number of sessions is dependent on the purpose of the group and the capacities and needs of the members. Until recent years, generally in social work, groups were planned for a relatively long duration of several months to a few years. More recently, there has been more focus on short-term groups. In working with children, often the most meaningful time period is the school semester or year. For most children, this is the time frame around which their lives are organized.

Periods of school vacations need to be taken into account when planning a group. It probably is not wise to start a group that is expected to meet once a week in late November or early December. In most school settings, there will be a Christmas vacation that will be disruptive, and perhaps destructive, to the beginning group stage. At the least, it would probably produce an unsettled condition for the group, producing regression in its development and in the behaviors of the members. Members may regress and start over, rather than build on the start that they had made up to that time. In groups, behaviors similar to those noted in the first few sessions, may be repeated and retried after returning from a vacation or a period of time away from the group. Children often return rather quickly to the manner in which they were interacting before vacation. At worst, the break may cause the group to disintegrate if it has not met enough times to develop an initial trust or cohesion.

At certain stages of the group, a short period of vacation away from the group may, if the consequences are worked through appropriately, act as a reenforcement to the group and its ongoing process. An example is as follows:

In a group of ten- and eleven-year-old girls who were in Stage III, "Working on My Goals and Those of Other Members," there was an interruption in services as the worker took her well-deserved annual vacation. For several sessions, the worker had advised the group that she would be gone for a short period of time and would be returning. The members seemed to have no problem with that; some girls almost seemed not to hear it or had the attitude of "why tell us?"

Upon the worker's return shortly thereafter, the group continued as usual with perhaps a little more tension than ordinary, but that was to be expected. Suddenly, toward the end of the session, one girl began to question in a hostile manner where the worker had been the previous week. Others began to join in. They, too, were obviously angry. The worker explained that she had told them that they would not meet those weeks. Had they forgotten? In response, the members asked what she had done during that time and stated that she did not like them anymore. After the worker offered reassurances about her care and concern for them, the members were able to express their anger and doubt and finally work through their feelings sufficiently to again believe the worker cared and could be trusted in the future. They could even express their anger at the worker, and still she assured them that she cared and would not reject them.

So, if breaks in the duration of sessions are well-timed and carefully worked through, they may, in fact, strengthen the relationships and trust in the group.

There is, however, probably a limit to the amount of time that most groups can refrain from meeting. Sometimes, children's groups attempt to stop meeting in the spring and then resume in the fall. Often the group has totally disbanded, and members have gone in many directions. Even if the majority of the members return, it is really similar to starting a new group and beginning again.

Another option that is sometimes attempted is to plan and conduct groups over the summer vacation. Often, this turns out to be a very inopportune time. Children may be involved with family vacations, visiting relatives and summer school or just be unwilling to schedule their time for a regular group session. The situation that may be an exception to this condition is a group that has a purpose of dealing with some type of crisis that the child is experiencing, such as a death of a significant other or a separation and divorce of parents.

Careful thought must be given to the purpose of the group in determining the duration. Sometimes, because of the nature of the problem that they have experienced, children can only tolerate a limited amount of focus at one time in attempting to work through new coping skills. In working with seriously physically abused children, it was found that a useful way of working was using a number of short-term groups over a period of time (Fatout, 1993). The children participated in a short-term group with the hope that they were able to stabilize and implement their gains. Then they were given opportunities to participate in another short-term group, often with different members.

If at all possible, it is important to plan for some flexibility in the duration of the group. One might decide to meet with the group for fifteen sessions, but at the end of ten, thirteen or even fifteen sessions, see compelling reasons to continue the group for another session or two. In working with children, the social worker will be actively guiding the pace and content of the sessions and, within limits, may have more control in attempting to help members meet their goals before termination.

Temporal Factors

Frequency, length and time are other factors that must be planned for in social work groups for children. *Frequency* is an especially important factor for children's groups. Often in working with groups, practitioners develop an expectation or "mind-set" that groups are to meet once a week for an hour or one and one-half hours. It is important to move from this expectation and really think about the potential group, its purpose and the possible length of the session. By "tuning in" as described by Schwartz (1971b), workers can begin to relate to the attitudes, thoughts and feelings of the potential members. This connection helps the workers develop an empathic perception of the possible situation experienced by the child and may assist them in more appropriately thinking about the frequency and length of the sessions.

It is also helpful for the worker to be aware of the developmental stage of the children as described in the previous chapter. Young latency age children can be expected to have a relatively short attention span. It may be more meaningful for the group to meet two or three times a week for a shorter period of time rather than once a week. This allows for more carry-over from one session to the next, making it more possible for the children to build on previous learning and experiences as they move toward goal accomplishment. (If a child, because of a short attention span and developmental stage, has difficulty remembering what happened in the last group session, there is little possibility of incorporating that experience for moving on.)

In some settings, such as residential treatment facilities and hospital wards where children are living together, groups sessions may be held every day. With the separation from their families and the anxiety that they may experience, frequency of meetings may help to alleviate some of their needs.

Basically, the *length of the session* is dependent on the purpose of the group and the capacity of the members to continue to interact. In a few instances where the children are extremely active and aggressive or exceedingly withdrawn, requiring an unusual amount of attention from the worker(s), the capacity and stamina of the practitioner(s) may need to be taken into account.

Group sessions for children often may be very short, perhaps fifteen to twenty minutes, and then be extended as the members are more able to tolerate longer time periods. Sometimes, it may be useful to vary the length of a session, perhaps once a month (but on a regular basis, so there is a predictability about it). This variance in the time period allows for differing content in the sessions and may help the group develop and members move toward goal attainment more rapidly (see example in Chapter 4).

External factors often affect the length of group sessions for children. If they are meeting at school during a class period, the session length is often controlled by the length of the class time. If the group is meeting after school, the time when it becomes dark outside, the weather, the time when parents are available to pick the children up and other such factors affect the length of the session.

In residential facilities, the length of a session may depend on when there is time in the daily schedule of the institution and when social workers are available to meet with the members. If the group meets in a clinic or other agency, many of the same factors described above may influence the length of sessions. In addition, usually there are few meeting rooms for children's groups, ones that are equipped and suitable (as described below), so careful scheduling may be necessary.

The *time of day* and *day of the week* are other factors to consider in planning. The parents and social worker will probably be concerned about not disrupting "important school subjects," while the child may often view those same times as most advantageous. Frequently, children see participation in a group as a special reward and sometimes use it to "get out of" classes in school. Some negotiations and careful planning must be done to select the most favorable time for everyone and one not disruptive to the educational experience.

It is important for the worker to be aware of how the time of day may to some extent influence the type of content suitable for use in group sessions. If the child has been sitting quietly for long periods of time, active content that allows for a great deal of physical movement may be essential, at least as the session starts. As an example, if the children have been sitting rather still for three or three and one-half hours, and it is right before lunch or just before school lets out, physical activity in the group is essential. However, if the children have just returned from recess or lunch, one would expect that they would be more ready for quiet, more sedentary group content.

If sessions are held in social agencies or settings away from school, this may present further stress and anxiety for children and their parents. The need for transportation and a longer period of time away from school may add to the pressure. It often becomes necessary for social workers to adjust their working schedule to be more available for evenings or weekends.

Space

Children are affected greatly by their external environment. It often provides stimulation for a great deal of physical activity. As noted by Churchill (1959), the arrangement and equipment present in a meeting room often pre-structures the content of that session (as described in more detail in Chapter 4). Because children, especially young children, have relatively short attention spans regardless of what has been planned for a session, their focus can be expected to be on the immediate environment, which, if not planned, can be very distracting.

Members' behaviors have been shown to be affected by the ways in which the chairs and tables are arranged in the meeting room (Churchill, 1959; Ward, 1968). These studies focused on work with adults, so it is unclear whether the effects are the same for children. It is easy, however, to imagine the different behavior of a group of seven- or eight-year-old children entering a meeting room with a table in the center surrounded by a straight back chair, in comparison to them entering a room with only large fluffy pillows. Obviously, the setting with the chairs and tables conveys an expectation of rather formal, disciplined behavior, probably with a task to be accomplished, while the pillows create the expectation of fun and relaxation.

The room for children's meetings needs to be large enough for members to sit together in a group for discussions and to push the chairs or equipment out of the way for more active participation. If the room is too small for utilizing it in this way, then an additional room or space elsewhere is needed for physical movement and games that are usually an essential component of children's groups.

Sometimes when the meeting room is very large, such as an auditorium or gym, it is important to provide limits and structure in verbal and nonverbal ways to help the children control their behavior enough to continue to participate in the group. (Some structuring and limiting techniques are described in Chapter 4.)

It is important to give some attention to the general appearance of the room, including colors and wall decorations that convey a liking and acceptance of children. Sometimes, safety is another area for attention in meeting rooms. For example, it may be necessary to have wire covers over the lights if the room is to be used for group activities.

The specific amount of space and arrangement of the room and its contents must be determined as much as possible by the age of the children, their problems and manner of expressing them, the purpose of the group, the content for focus in a session and other factors that can only be determined by the worker. Probably the greatest reality factor is that because of lack of space, for example in a school setting, groups often meet wherever there is a place available.

Many compromises may need to be made between the reality of the situation and ideal conditions. However, there are some conditions that are really impossible for meeting rooms for groups. Areas that may not be real possibilities for meetings may be the teacher's lounge, with teachers continuously coming and going, or the band room. The situation with the band room is described as follows:

A group in a school setting was given the band room for its meetings. All types of band instruments were everywhere in the room. The children were curious and wanted to play with the instruments. In order to protect the equipment, the attention of the social worker was almost always on this issue. There was no time to focus on the problems/needs that originally brought the group together. It was essential to find another setting.

Composition

Careful consideration of the characteristics of members who compose the group is important. As noted by Bertcher and Maple (1977, p. 7), "It is our impression that many people overlook or underestimate the powerful effect of a group's composition on the interaction that ensues." It is generally agreed by those in the profession that at minimum it is important that members have a broad commonality of purpose.

A great deal of research has been conducted regarding the selection of members into a configuration that will be most productive (Glick & Jackson, 1970; Hare, 1962; Hartford, 1972; McGrath & Altman, 1966; Shaw, 1971). Henry (1992) states that conclusions regarding composition are inconclusive or contradictory. She further asserts that, at best, selecting group members is "guess work" (Henry, 1992, p. 4).

Experience suggests that her conclusions are more applicable to adult groups than to children's groups. By looking at specific factors in composing children's groups, it is possible to avoid a catastrophe, a dysfunctional group or at least a major conflict that may prove destructive to the group.

The conclusions from practice knowledge and wisdom ascertained by Hartford (1972) and further elaborated on by Bertcher and Maple (1978) have often been found to be most applicable to forming groups for children.

Factors that are especially important in forming groups of children are commonality of purpose, age and sex. The one exception to this is the short-term group. If the purpose of the group is very specific and focused, and the duration of the group is short, neither age nor sex may be of great importance.

The significance of having similar problems has been described above and is generally true for all age groups. The factor that is most crucial in developing groups for children is age or, often more specifically stated, their developmental stage. Because children move through developmental stages so rapidly, it is important in composing a group to be aware of the developmental tasks that are of uppermost importance for a particular child. Probably, except when there are serious developmental lags, a two-year age difference is a workable range for membership in children's groups. So, six- and seven-year-olds can probably be included in the same group, or seven- and eight-year-olds together.

There may be a period of time when looking very carefully at the developmental level is essential in composing a group of girls. It is the time when they are moving from latency to preadolescence, probably between the ages of eleven to twelve years. During this age period, their interests often change rapidly from childish play to teenage concerns such as boys and social occasions. Often, hair styles and type of dress are important clues in assessing the girls' stage of development. Having a group composed of girls with very divergent interests becomes an almost impossible situation for the social worker. This has not been found to be as true in working with boys, as they seem to be able to move back and forth across areas of interest.

Sex of members may be another very important factor to consider in planning a group. Ordinarily, boys and girls from school-age to adolescence do not choose to be together for extended periods of time. Their interests are often very different, and there are periods of time when boys "don't like girls" and when girls "cannot stand boys." It is probably important to take these feelings into consideration in forming a group. If boys and girls are to be included in the same group, it is important to be able to state reasons why it is appropriate and workable. Groups of latency age children are often put together in a school setting with male and female co-leaders. This may work for the first few sessions, but soon workers may decide to split the group—the girls with the female worker and the boys with the male worker—because of the great differences in interest of the sexes.

Two other areas of concern in composing a group for children are what might be called the "sink or swim" and the "no one of a kind" rules. It is very important that children who are already having serious problems relating to others not be placed in a group where they can not succeed. An illustration of this is a group of children who are having behavior problems in the classroom:

Most of the members selected to participate are very outgoing or aggressive; others either cannot stay in their seats, are "daydreamers" or nonparticipating students. Donnie, who is very quiet and often withdrawn, is also perceived by the teacher as having problems in participating appropriately. It is decided that he could gain something from participation, and the others "might learn something" from him. After a session or two in the group, instead of Donnie improving, he became more frightened and refused to return to the group.

To have included Donnie in the group is of necessity a worker's decision, but must be carefully thought through. The worker in this case seems to have used the "sink or swim" rule—"he will either make it or he won't"—or the worker has simply made a bad judgment. The result is a child who probably is having more problems than before and may not want to ever participate in peer groups again.

The other area for cautious consideration is not including any *one* child who is viewed as different from the others in some way that is important to the rest of the group. It is difficult for workers to be aware of this unless they know the attitudes and beliefs of the communities from which the children come. In some communities or neighborhoods, a difference, such as being Italian, Protestant, "Anglo" or many other specific designations, may make the child unacceptable to the others. If a child who is viewed in this way is to be included, then at least two or more with this characteristic should also be incorporated into the group. This way, the one child does not immediately become the scapegoat, and the group is given the opportunity to work out the differences between members.

In summary, a large number of decisions must be made in planning for a group. Sometimes, this may be seen as a tedious process but, as was indicated previously, it may make the difference between a successful group and one that does not survive or is a negative experience for the members.

RECRUITMENT AND INTAKE OF CHILDREN

Methods for recruitment of members may vary from one group to another depending on the purpose of the group. One commonly used method in social work settings is that of referrals. This process has been described previously. After having been alerted to the needs of a partic ular child, it generally includes at least one interview with the child previous to the determination of the composition of the group. The worker is looking for a number of children who have enough commonalities to be comfortable together, and yet enough differences that they can become a viable group (Redl, 1944).

Another commonly used procedure for recruitment for children's groups is advertising that a group will be formed. Posters may be placed in the neighborhood telling the time and place of the first session. Using this method of forming groups usually does not involve the use of pre-group interviews.

Determining which of these two methods of recruitment is most appropriate is dependent on the purpose that the group is to serve. If the purpose of the group is to focus on a particular need or problem, such as divorce of parents, problematic classroom behavior, physical abuse or other specific concerns, then there is a need for some sort of discrete screening that puts the worker in contact with these children, which is most often accomplished through referrals. If, however, the group has a purpose of helping children with the tasks of a particular developmental stage or with an issue common to those children living in the community, such as violence, drugs or other community-wide problems, then a poster at a neighborhood grocery store or community center may be appropriate. It could simply state, for example, that a group for third-grade boys is being organized, and indicate the time and place.

The commonality of members' problems in the referred group can be expected to be specific and more amenable to immediate focus by the worker and the group. In contrast, the group recruited by the use of posters, can be expected to be experiencing a variety of problems, and more time may be needed to focus and prioritize issues of concern for these members. Often, a concern in working with a group formed using this latter method is the lack of control the worker has over the final composition of the group. When children come to the first session, unless several groups are being formed concurrently, it may be necessary because of their numbers to turn away some of them or offer some other alternatives.

Notifying Potential Members of the Group

When referrals are used and group composition has been determined, the next step may be to notify the children of the beginning of the group. There are several options that must be considered when doing this. A letter may be sent or a phone call made, or the referral source may notify the potential members. There may be pros and cons of each of these alternatives that must be considered and taken into account as the process continues.

A letter to a special group (or party), if it has the qualities of an invitation, may be very enticing. Or, if it seems too formal, may be seen as threatening and coming from someone in authority. For some children, simply having the invitation on paper to hold in their hands and look at enhances the excitement and anticipation of their upcoming experience.

A phone call may at first seem exciting for some or frightening to others, partially dependent on previous experiences with authority figures. In addition, after the phone call is finished, there may be questions that are unanswered or unclear, and there is not a reminder available for the child as there is with the letter. This method is often the quickest and easiest, but it may seem unplanned to the child and his/her parents.

A third option is for the referring source to tell the members about the group. In this case, the worker and the potential group may be greatly influenced by the way in which this is done. The results may either be positive or negative. An illustration of this is a vice-principal in a school who referred seven boys for a group. He selected those that he saw most often because of their creating problems in the school setting. He then told them that a group was being formed that they should attend. The natural assumption is that this group is intended to provide more "punishment" for their behaviors. So, even though they have had individual interviews with the worker, this message from the vice-principal again reinforces the belief that they are in trouble. If the boys arrive (at all) to the first session, they can be expected to be hostile and untrusting of the worker and situation. Often, an outside source simply cannot communicate accurately about the purpose and content of the group.

Another issue that needs thinking through and planning is whether parents should be notified about the group before, at the same time or after the children are informed. In order to make the most appropriate judgment, some thinking about the developmental stage of the children involved and their level of sophistication are important areas to consider. If children are in a developmental stage in which they are desperately attempting to separate themselves (psychologically) from parents and reaching out to peers, the worker would want to notify the children first, followed a short time later with information to the parents. In contrast, if a group was being formed for seven-year-olds, the worker might decide that it would be most advantageous to communicate with the parents of the prospective members first. (Children of this age generally want close parental involvement in what they are doing.) This could give the parents information, answer their questions and begin to develop trust regarding the services that are being offered to their child. In every case, regardless of the child's age, it is important to consider what the parents might expect from the worker and perhaps the expected timing of that communication.

Other Areas for Planning

This timing of communication with the parents is important, because it often creates some expectations on the part of the children in regard to confidentiality. It is important in developing a therapeutic group atmosphere that children be allowed to communicate freely without fear of reprimands or "trouble" from persons outside the group, especially parents and teachers.

The area of confidentiality is an especially difficult one in working with children. Young children, because of their development stage and relationship with parents, may tell their parents everything that happened during the day, thus setting a norm of confidentiality may not be very realistic. Even at this young age, children do know about "secrets" and seem to enjoy them. This concept is probably the most meaningful for preteen children. A statement that has been very useful in discussions of this concern has been, "I will not tell people outside the group things that will get you into trouble, I am here to help you stay out of trouble." After they understand that position, it is also important that they be assured that you may find it important to tell others if they are doing something to hurt themselves or others. If at all possible, however, you will let them know before this is done and perhaps invite them to join you in discussions with parents or teachers. These types of comments seems to alleviate some of the children's fears and concerns and, at the same time, help them feel protected (that the worker will not let them get out of control).

A final area for planning is the content of the first group session. A general format for the group was determined earlier, now the specific content needs to be planned. It is important to state the purpose of the group and invite discussion of that statement by the members. This process allows for the beginning development of trust, as the members can identify that the worker is again stating to the whole group the same purpose that was discussed in the individual interview. Inviting members' discussion of the purpose is intended to convey to the children that they have some power and influence in this group and some ability to influence the process expected to occur.

A question always of concern to children is, "What are we going to do in here?" The worker must be prepared to answer this in some way and hopefully to guide them in a discussion of their ideas about this subject. As identified in Chapter 1, the social worker aids the children in becoming a group. This involves the worker often taking the "host/hostess" role in connecting children by introducing them as they arrive and having some plan for activities that promote their getting acquainted. Refreshments are often used to help social interactions occur.

It is important for the worker to put thought into developing some continuity between this session and the next one. It is often helpful to summarize what the group has accomplished this day, and the things the members might wish to do in the future, perhaps suggesting things to do at the next session. This allows children to feel that the next session will not be totally unpredictable, and that some things are already known by them.

Planning for the group is perhaps one of the most tedious and difficult tasks for the worker, because of the many unknown factors and the variety of judgments that must be made. Once this is accomplished, the group and its work and purposeful fun with the children is about to begin. The ease of moving into work with the children can be expected to be much greater with the planning that has been accomplished to this time. Planning will continue, but now the focus will be on creating a group, assessing the members and helping them move toward their goals.

This process of planning prepares the worker and the members to build a culture where changes can be made and goals accomplished. Especially in working with children, it is important to allow them some share of the power, so that the group really becomes theirs. This power and control must be ceded gradually and purposefully by the practitioner, as the members and the group, as a whole, are ready to assume it. Readiness for this experience requires maturation in terms of both individual and group development (as described in previous chapters). Primary procedures for initiating and carrying out this process are described and illustrated in the following chapters.

Chapter 4
Developing a Mutual Aid System

A fundamental concern and focus of the practitioner in working with a group of any age is creating a mutual aid system. This emphasis continues throughout the duration of the group up to the termination stage. The primary agent of change in the group is the group itself. "As members reach out to each other, they experience a variety of helping relationships and become increasingly invested in each other and in participating in interpersonal processes" (Gitterman, 1989, p. 6). People grow and change as they relate to others, partly through the processes of give-and-take. Relationships are enhanced as individuals find that not only can they receive from others, but they also have something to give to others. This give-and-take process may reduce members' feelings of inadequacy or differences, inability to cope and dependence on the social worker.

Alissi (1981) summarized this process by stating that "the hallmark of the social work group process is evidenced in the ability to recognize the power that resides in the small group, to help members harness this power to meet personal needs and to achieve socially constructive purposes" (p. 714). As mutual support develops, members dare to struggle with their real issues; now the others are genuinely accepting and are able to offer hope, because affective ties have developed between them. The concept of mutual aid helps to define a primary role of the worker—to facilitate the members in helping one another to achieve individual and collective aspirations. Mutual aid requires that certain attitudes and feelings be established. It is essential that members' defensiveness diminish and that trust and intimacy increase. Much of what the worker does is aimed at stimulating the members to use the resources available to them within the group, and in the agency and community.

MUTUAL AID WITH CHILDREN

This view of the group as a reciprocal helping system is very important in working with children who are in the process of learning to participate in the broader world of extrafamilial groups. By developing mutually responsible interaction among members, the growth of each member is promoted as well as the cohesion of the total group (Zayas & Lewis, 1986). Obviously, young children, because of lack of experience, will not have as many resources available to them within the group as one might expect with older children or adults. It becomes essential that the social worker participate very actively, helping children make connections with each other, participating with them and guiding them in developing this helping system.

Procedures for Developing Mutual Aid

A major focus for the worker throughout the life of the group, at least until Stage IV, "We Prepare Ourselves and End the Group," is developing a mutual aid system. The beginning stages are very centered on developing a group in which members both give and receive assistance from each other. Yalom (1985) describes this process as "culture building." Group culture includes values, beliefs, customs and traditions that the group members hold in common (Olmsted, 1959). As the children come to the group, they all bring and "contribute their unique sets of values that originate from their past experience as well as from their ethnic, cultural and racial heritages" (Toseland & Rivas, 1994, p. 84). Through communication and interaction, the children explore each other's unique value systems during the early group stages. With some knowledge and understanding of commonalities and differences, a group culture begins to emerge and develops throughout the first four group stages.

Basic Procedures and Techniques

Within social work, some of the methods used to develop culture have been identified. The typology developed by Northen (1988), based on a content analysis of major books on social work practice and on the research conducted by Fatout (1975) of several other social workers, is a very useful one to employ in working with children. The word *procedure* refers to a particular course of action or manner of intervening in a process. "A technique is a set of specific interrelated actions that carries out the intent of a procedure" (Northen, 1988, p. 56).

A procedure that is especially helpful in working with children is that of *using structure*. (Many descriptions of ways to implement this procedure are depicted in Chapter 5.) It is believed that the use of this method can help empower members by shifting the locus of control from outside to within themselves.

Another major procedure that is used with children throughout the life of the group is giving *support*. This may be focused on a member, a sub-group or the group as a whole. The intent of this procedure is to enhance a sense of self-esteem and security. Support is often used to maintain or enhance the current level of functioning. The target of this procedure may be differing levels of systems; for instance, the worker's supportive statement may be addressed to one member but also be intended to convey a message to the total group. An example of this type of worker statement is, "Mary, we really have missed you for the last two weeks." In making this statement, the worker intends to convey the supportive message that the group cares about Mary and is aware that she was not present for two weeks.

Another target of this message may be the total group. The worker may be attempting to convey to all members that they are a group and they care when any member is not present. More specifically, the worker may be supporting the development or maintenance of cohesion in the group. In this process of giving support, the worker is actively modeling a behavior that is desirable for members to adopt. Modeling seems to be an especially appropriate method for broadening the experience and learning of children, since it is a technique that is utilized by them during their developmental stage (as described in Chapter 2). It is expected that, as the group progresses and the children have learned to give support, they will use this procedure as a means of providing mutual support for each other.

Some specific techniques often used to convey support with children are: holding a child on one's lap, putting an arm around a child's shoulder if indicated, making a point of sitting next to a child, holding his/her hand if desired by the child, giving a child attention and making some statement to him/her. Sometimes children need more attention and support than the worker is able to give. This occurred in a group of children who had been seriously abused.

When Jimmie entered the group, he had been withdrawn and carefully stayed away from and out of the reach of the worker. Gradually, as he began to trust her, he became very demanding of her attention, first wanting to sit next to her and later wishing to sit on her lap or to snuggle up as an infant with as much contact with her as possible. (This was a group with two workers and only five members, so there were many opportunities for contacts with the workers.) As the meeting ended, the worker stood with Jimmie next to her. Another member came over to talk with her. The group had been served refreshments and were still drinking their punch. When the worker diverted her attention away from Jimmie, he carefully began to pour a measured amount of the drink on her skirt. The purpose of this seemed to be two-fold: to regain her attention even in a negative manner and to test his relationship with her.

Obviously, support in many forms was essential to the functioning and growth of this child, and he was testing to see if he would be rejected. He had learned of some negative ways to ask for attention, but now was at least trusting enough to take a risk.

Especially with older children, supportive techniques that may be particularly useful are: encouraging, recognizing a contribution a member has made, expressing hope, giving reassurance and expressing realistic expectations.

Exploration involves another set of techniques that is important in working with children. The purpose of using these techniques is to bring feelings, opinions and facts out into the open. For children who are moving from a family environment into a community environment, it is especially important that they gain broader understanding about how others in society think and feel. "It is assumed that, as people disclose more about themselves and their situation to others, they reveal themselves not only to others but also to themselves, which sets in motion a process of clarification" (Northen, 1988, p. 61).

Some of the exploration techniques used are: eliciting information and feelings, purposeful inquiry, asking questions and making comments to guide the members. Often, children have not thought about the reasons behind beliefs or actions. As the worker wonders why something happened as it did, the child is given the opportunity to explore, question and clarify reasons behind feelings, thoughts and situations and search for alternative decisions and explanations.

In working with children, another procedure that is emphasized is *education* or *advice*. For children, there are many new things to learn as they more actively enter the community and the world outside the family. The purpose of education is to provide them with knowledge and skills for coping with different situations. Social workers have an opportunity to provide information to children in a variety of ways. Through game playing, they may teach children to label the feelings that they are experiencing. Through the use of discussion and receiving feedback from others, they may learn how to request information from others that they need. Sometimes information giving by the worker is done very indirectly:

A situation in which this indirect method was used was with a group of children who were available for adoption. The workers believed it was essential to educate them about how "non-abusive families" functioned. In order to accomplish this, the workers used storytelling with a family represented by figures cut from magazines. First the workers told stories, then they encouraged members to talk about this family.

This activity, in the guise of entertainment, was a way to give information to the children about how "normal" mothers, fathers and children function in families.

Suggestions and advice are other techniques that may be used to educate. Special care must be used in the manner and conditions in which these techniques can be useful for the child. Children may totally ignore advice or become resentful or more dependent if this technique is not used thoughtfully. If the suggestions or advice are really what children need, it can be very helpful and useful for them. For example, if the child is having difficulty communicating with a teacher about a grade received at school, it may be because of the way that the child is expressing him/herself. A discussion with the total group about alternative ways to ask the question and then role-playing to help the child become more comfortable with a new way of communicating, may provide a different approach for getting the desired information.

Confrontation is another procedure used with children. Its purpose is to interrupt or reverse the course of action. Confrontations are direct statements, but they need not be harsh. As noted by Overton and Tinker (1957), they can be a "firm challenge with an arm around the shoulder" (p. 68).

A type of confrontation often used in working with children is one that is intended to stop behavior. Children may begin to fight or play in a manner that is too rough. The confrontation may take the form of statements by the practitioner, such as "I can't let you fight or continue to play like that. I don't want either of you to get hurt." This certainly could be identified as a "gentle confrontation." These comments encompass two of the procedures, confrontation and support. (As has been noted in the literature [Fatout, 1975], confrontation is often supplemented by the use of support.)

Another form of confrontation that is often used with children is a statement that is intended to make children aware of the discrepancies between what they say and what they are doing. For example, "You told me your goal was to make better grades in school, but now you tell me you are not doing your homework. I wonder how that will affect things."

As the group progresses to a later stage, children often begin to confront each other, sometimes not too gently. However, if the worker has modeled confrontation supplemented by support, children soon begin to use some of these methods. In situations where the member-to-member confrontation is too harsh, the worker can often provide the supportive behavior that allows the confrontation to remain useful. An example is a child who confronted another member by saying, "You always cause trouble for us." The worker quickly responded, "He doesn't always misbehave. Sometimes he does some very nice things. What is he doing now that seems bothersome? Maybe we can talk about this together." In this way, the worker takes an accusatory statement and shifts it to a gentle confrontation.

A final procedure used by the worker is *clarification*. The techniques are used to promote the members' understanding of themselves and situations. It is assumed that as children come to understand and perceive themselves and/or others differently, behaviors, feelings and attitudes are also altered. The very development of a mutual aid system depends on a group environment in which there is clarity in communication between the members. To accomplish this, the worker models sending messages that are clear and congruent and listens to the members with understanding and sensitivity. Participation by all of the members is invited. The worker scans the group and displays supportive behaviors both verbally and nonverbally. This is intended to convey that there is an expectation and a hope that all members will share with the others as they feel the desire to do so. The worker continues to help members clarify themselves by redirecting messages to others in the group, remaining silent to produce participation by others, restating major points, asking for amplification of details and promoting the use of words that transmit feelings of identity with the group.

Other techniques often used are: helping members find explanations for behaviors, allowing members to discuss taboo subjects, helping members make connections between events and broadening the alternative for interpretation of them and providing further information for the group's discussion. All of these worker behaviors are intended to help members further understand themselves and others and also to learn the skills and ways of thinking that may allow them to continue to do this in the future. These procedures are very basic to the development of a cohesive group and a "culture" that becomes a mutual aid system for all of the members.

Skills Specific to Developing Mutual Aid

Processes, as they develop naturally in the group, are essential to a therapeutic system. Some very specific assumptions underlie the concept of a mutual aid system. "People need each other and the social groupings of which they are a part; there is no wholeness or real existence in isolation" (Lee & Swenson, 1986, p. 362). The group is viewed as a helping system in which members need each other and the worker. Furthermore, it is believed that change resides in the client not in the helper.

Gitterman (1989) has identified specific skills that are intended to support and promote this essential helping system.

Directing members' transactions to each other. The use of this skill reinforces the development of a belief that all members have the ability to both take from the group and give to the group and each other; that the members of the group can become the resource for everyone else as needed. Answers to problems and situations that members are experiencing do not reside with the worker or someone outside the group but are available from others in the system.

An instance of this occurred when Tim asked the worker, "Why does everyone pick on me?" The worker responded, "I'm not sure I know the answer to that. Maybe you should ask that question of the group." The worker continued, "Bill looks like he has something to say."

Helping the members make connections with each other and identifying potential assets that members have are essential to the evolution of a helping network.

Inviting members to build on the contributions of others. Often this process involves the practitioner's intervention by asking the group for feedback on a member's ideas. "Louise suggested that it would be fun to go skating. What do the rest of you think of that idea?" Or as Louise makes the suggestion and others immediately respond, "Yeah, let's do that," the worker reminds them that "we will have to plan how we can do this."

Reinforcing the norms of mutual support and assistance. An example of this happened in a group of seven- and eight-year-old boys who were in the "getting acquainted stage." The group members had decided to draw a mural that represented their interests as a club that could be put on the wall for others to see. Troy had been very quiet and withdrawn in the group until this session. As it immediately became evident, art was the area in which he excelled. He soon completed his area of the mural and looked around for other things to draw.

Jason was struggling to draw an airplane and had been asking the worker for assistance. The worker suggested that maybe Troy could draw "good" planes. With that, Jason indicated he wanted Troy's help. After the mural was completed, the practitioner said the children really acted like a group today by sharing crayons and ideas about what and how to draw things. In addition, they had discovered that some of the members have some special talents that can help the group in the future. "They should feel proud of their club."

In this example, the members were all discovering that they could work successfully together by sharing and assisting others, and that members often have special talents or skills that can be useful to the whole group.

Developing common group sanctions. Before members really become comfortable in relating to each other, it is essential that they come to some agreement about ways of talking and behaving in their group. "When members are clear about what behaviors are preferred, permitted, proscribed and prohibited, they are likely to be less anxious and more available to each other" (Gitterman, 1989, p. 13).

The worker often plays a very important role in helping the group deal with this issue. The concern of the social worker is not to limit language and behavior so that children are inhibited in their ability to express themselves. At the same time, however, if a manner of behaving or talking is not acceptable to all of the members, then perhaps it is not appropriate for this group. An example of this follows:

A group of older latency girls lived in a low-income neighborhood. Many of their older siblings were involved in gang activities, and some of their parents had been gang members earlier in their lives. The group members had been exposed to words and behaviors in their neighborhood that were not acceptable to the community at large. In order to allow the girls to freely express themselves, the worker and members agreed that they could talk in the clubroom as they wished, but with the public in the general community much of this communication and behavior was not acceptable. A concern of the worker was whether the girls would know what was not appropriate behavior in the community. However, if these girls were going to function in the larger community, it was important that they be clear about what was acceptable. During the second stage of the group, "Establishing My Place," members or the group as a whole often tested the boundaries of tolerable behavior both within and outside of the clubroom.

In one particular instance, the group went together to a park in the community. There were also many other community people there. Some of the girls began to use their clubroom talk and behaviors in that setting. The behavior of a few members was contagious, and soon all of them were participating in similar ways. The worker insisted that the group return to the van so they could return to the clubroom. They had tested the limits that they had established earlier; now further clarification and agreement were important. In the discussion that ensued, the limits of behavior were further established.

It is from this type of testing, exploring, trials and discussion that parameters of approved or disapproved group behaviors are established. Often, the testing and trial of behavior is done in a much more subtle manner than is illustrated here.

Encouraging collective action and activities. When members experience things together, they may create a supportive mutual atmosphere. Experiencing together can be a part of the ongoing process in the group.

For example, much of the planning and decision-making that is essential to a group involves this type of activity. As the group follows through on plans and experiences success, there is further development of trust, belief in others and feeling supported in and by the total group.

In addition to these naturally occurring processes in the group, the practitioner may purposefully develop a program that provides opportunities for members to participate in activities that assist in the development of a mutual aid system. Zayas and Lewis (1986) describe the use of the game "Dungeons and Dragons" as a means for assisting the group to generate a helping network. The authors note that

by posing real or imaginary dilemmas that call for group problem-solving the worker naturally exposes the group to such aspects of mutual aid as the identification of common problems, and tasks necessitated, division of labor with assigned roles and functions, and the formulation of a strategy for attaining the groups' goals. (1986, p. 54)

Role-playing activities, which have used similar interventions and methods, are stories such as *Star Trek* that can provide a variety of roles and situations to problem-solve.

Clarifying members task and role responsibilities. By being clear about the division of labor, each member becomes aware of the specific task that every other member is to perform and of the part that task plays in the total success of the group's activity. If the group has planned to cook hot dogs in the park, and the member responsible for bringing the buns does not perform his/her task, it negatively affects the total group. Each member recognizes that all of the others are depending on his/her performance on the assigned tasks.

Structuring collective decision-making. If the children are unable to make a decision, it may be necessary to provide a structure within which they are able to reach an agreement. Often in groups, a round robin is used in which each child, in turn, is allowed to give one idea. This gives opportunities for all to participate regardless of their status in the group as well as a beginning structure for decision-making. As the process continues and members run out of new ideas, those ideas that have been recorded are looked at again to eliminate duplication and impractical alternatives. From this structured beginning, the members are able to communicate, interact and come to a decision. This process helps members learn to listen to each other and give support to ideas and others.

Identifying and focusing on salient group themes. Throughout the life of the group, common themes emerge and subside. In a group of members who were living in foster homes, the children began to talk about their general experiences in school and with peers. The worker clarified by saying, "I wonder if all of you have difficulty explaining why your names are different from that of your parents?" As the children agreed with this, they realized that they were "all in the same boat," experiencing the same kinds of feelings. It is important in developing mutuality that members recognize their common feelings and thoughts. The worker's comments about this in the group help members become more conscious of their common concerns. As the worker looks for and identifies these common themes, a helping network continues to emerge.

Reaching for discrepant perceptions and opinions. It is important that the practitioner understands that all members may not be in agreement about an idea, belief or decision. Sometimes this lack of agreement is hidden by the silence of the dissenting member. It is important that the worker be aware of this difference of opinion and bring it into the open. As noted by Gitterman (1989), "A collective is only as strong as its ability to allow and tolerate differences. Members can only be supportive of each other, if they feel sufficient comfort to state their thoughts and feelings openly" (p. 15).

Inviting all members to participate. Because of their differing ethnic, cultural and family backgrounds, not all children participate at the same rate. Some, because of personality differences, may not wish to speak in front of the group. These differences may represent established differences, or they may be due to the nature of the content or the presence or absence of certain other members. Sometimes in early group sessions, it may be observed that one member never speaks aloud, participating through a more vocal member. This is often accomplished by elbow nudges or an aside to a adjacent friend, who then vocalizes the feeling or idea to the group.

The invitation to participate must be done by the worker with great care, sensitivity and understanding. It is important that silent members are not ignored but rather know that their participation is welcome when they are ready to enter into the interacting process. This message can continually be reinforced by the worker, purposefully making eye contact and being aware of the silent members' nonverbal communication while scanning the group for responses. This alerts the worker to when the member is really involved in the discussion and seems to have something to contribute, so that the practitioner may comment that the member seems to have something to say. This may provide the opportunity and proper timing for the member to make a first attempt.

Sometimes the lack of participation has been taught at home. In one instance, a girl was very outgoing, boisterous and somewhat aggressive in interacting with the group. As she found herself in close proximity to the worker and only a few members to protect and buffer her and her participation, she became very withdrawn and silent. This behavior was noted over a period of time. Even when the worker said to her that it had been a nice day, the girl became very quiet and very guarded in her response to such a neutral statement. After continuing to explore this behavior, the worker wondered aloud why the girl did not want to talk with her. The girl's response was very clear. She had been told by her mother not to discuss "family business" in the group. She had evidently been feeling a great deal of pressure about this and attempting to determine when it was alright to participate and when it was not. She had determined it was alright to partic- ipate freely with the members, but communication directly with the practitioner was a violation of her mother's rules. In order to free the girl to participate, it was necessary to go back to the mother and reinterpret the group as one which was not intended to get members and their families in trouble but rather to help them stay out of difficulties.

It is intended that the worker's seeking each member's participation is to model and convey a belief in the importance of each member's contribution to the group.

Creating emotional and physical space for individual members. Members of groups have differing needs in regard to their separateness, space and timing in participation. It is important that the worker respect and model this belief for other group members. As members feel more accepted and understood, they become freer and more comfortable in participating in the group. This leads to more investment and commitment to the group and the other members and thus to a greater depth in feelings of mutual aid. On occasion, this may mean supporting members who do not want to participate with the others or to discuss a specific subject on a partic- ular day. It involves a respect for individuals and their special needs and desires, which is intended to convey acceptance of the individual by other group members.

SUMMARY

The worker must very actively participate and guide the development of a mutual aid system. First, by using procedures and techniques throughout the life of the group that are intended to build a group cul- ture and also by employing specific worker skills to further shape and develop that helping system.

There is such a range of ability and coping skills in childhood, that the social worker must continually be aware of the individual member's level of development and capacity to use a mutual aid system. Sometimes, the worker must be the connecting link between members within that system. As Goldstein (1981) describes it, "The leader's com- mitments provide a measure of support and reassurance that can be borrowed until such time as the group itself comes to take on significance in the perceptions of its members" (p. 329).

Sometimes the practitioner may teach the group to cultivate a helping system by posing real or imaginary dilemmas that require group problem-solving. In doing this, the members are naturally exposed to problem identification, a plan for a division of labor with assigned roles and functions and formulation of a strategy to attain goals. This learning of a process for mutual problem-solving is often derived from simply functioning in a group. There are often decisions that must be made for a children's group to function. By including children in the process, they soon learn the advantages of working together. Out of these experiences emerge feelings of worth and purpose. The altruistic self finds that it can extend help to others as well as receive help from others. The importance of this learning is reinforced by Northen (1988, p. 25), "The way in which persons relate to each other is the heart of the group process."

This chapter described the development of a helping network as a major process essential to work with children. Another important mechanism to help children make changes is the use of limits and structures as a means of empowering them to try alternative behaviors. These are described in the following chapter.

Chapter 5

Therapeutic Use of Settings and Other Limiting Structures

After planning, recruiting and forming a group, a culture must be established to serve as a therapeutic medium for the children. The goal of the worker is to establish a mutual aid system that will allow the children to function together while working on individual and group goals. In order to accomplish this end, a variety of procedures and skills are used by the social worker to develop and intervene in group interaction. While a caring relationship is developing between the social worker and the members, it is essential to use both verbal and nonverbal acts to assist members and the group to move toward their goals. Often these interventions are called techniques. Procedures are comprised of clusters of these techniques, which are intended to move toward a course of action.

Social workers with groups have labeled and described these procedures and techniques in many ways (Fatout, 1975; Northen, 1969, 1988; Smalley, 1970; Trecker, 1948). The classification developed by Fatout (1975) and later elaborated on by Northen (1988) will be used as the basis for this chapter. Fatout (1975) found in searching the literature that social work intervention could be categorized into six types of procedures. The major procedures or clusters of techniques are support, exploration, confrontation, education-advice, clarification and structuring.

In working with children, structuring is an especially useful and meaningful procedure for developing the group and helping members move toward goal accomplishment. Because of the developmental stage children and their need to learn new ways of relating and experiencing the world, the use of structure is essential in providing a situation in which there are boundaries but still space for exploration.

The use of limits in working with children can be an empowering process for them. Limits or structures can define the boundaries of acceptable actions, permitting the child a range of possible behaviors within which to experiment. Because children are growing and maturing, there are certain tasks to be accomplished before they move on to the next stage of psychosocial development. Structuring permits the child to accomplish these tasks in a safer, more controlled manner.

Especially for latency age children, the social work group can provide an atmosphere that promotes play and fantasy while interacting with a group of peers. As described in the previous chapter, children can begin to prepare to interact with the broader society from an empowered position. Through this process, they acquire cultural behavior patterns, beliefs and rituals that will guide their opinions, mores and interactions throughout life.

EXTERNAL STRUCTURES AND LIMITS

All of society functions within some form of structure, whether it is the law, mores of the community or rules of the family. The social worker, by becoming aware of those limits or structures affecting the group members, may be able to make more purposeful use of them.

Purpose

Usually children's groups are conducted in and under the auspices of an agency that is located in the community. The organizers of that facility had very definite purposes in mind when that agency was established. As Garvin (1981, p. 39) notes, "The agency purpose for the group will have a strong influence on group processes throughout the life of the group." Some specific areas affected will be who is referred to the group; how the person is prepared, if at all, for the experience; what kind of group activities are used; what subjects or issues are emphasized; and what agency resources are made available to the group for utilization.

Obviously, if the agency's purpose, for example, is to work with delinquency-prone children, the primary persons making referrals are the principals or vice-principals in the schools. These are the authority figures most often in contact with the child who is having problems of this type. Since this is the agency's purpose, it has the personnel and resources to work with this type of child. Over time, the agency gains a reputation for working with a specific variety of population. In the organization noted above, its prominence in the delinquency area was so well known that former members referred new members, or individuals often referred themselves.

Special attention may be used in preparing children to participate in this type of group. There are two basic considerations in thinking about recruitment and composition. One is the specific method of recruitment, the other is the resulting composition of the group. It must be determined how and if contact is to be made with the children previous to the first group session. Will individual conferences be scheduled and conducted? Will casual contacts be made with the children at recess? Will parents be contacted or not contacted at all? The nature of the population to be served (older latency age children in this example) suggests that the less formal contact is most productive. As Northen (1969, p. 106) states, "informality tends to reduce social distance between staff and clientele."

The other concern of the worker in recruiting members is the mutual fit of the individuals with each other in the group. So, the commonalities and differences must be noted that are believed to enhance functioning of groups for this purpose.

Activities and emphasis in program would be focused on helping members resolve problems in more socially acceptable ways rather than resorting to delinquent acts for resolution. In doing this, the agency would be expected to provide resources to make this focus feasible.

As can be seen in this example, the agency's purpose is a most important structure that determines many factors related to the group. The social worker must be very clear about the purpose of the agency and the degree of flexibility therein, before it is utilized as a host setting.

Location and Reputation of the Agency

Other limits or structures that may affect the potential group member are the name of the agency, its geographic location and its reputation in the neighborhood. Obviously, the geographic location and the reputation of the organization is going to affect the participation of the child. If it is seen to be located in an unacceptable neighborhood or if the child must walk through "rough" areas to reach the group, the child may not be allowed to participate regardless of the reputation of the program. On the other hand, even though the neighborhood is acceptable, if the agency has a "bad" reputation, participation may be curtailed by the parents. In some instances, even though the organization's policies in regard to race, ethnicity, religion and other discriminatory factors are very broad, the agency's name, in itself, may prevent some from participating. For example, some parents may prevent their non-Jewish child from participating in a group held in a Jewish agency.

STRUCTURE AND LIMITS WITHIN THE GROUP

There are also some limits or structures within the group that can be effectively utilized to promote the autonomy and power of the child.

Format

The format or structure of the use of time within the session may be used to communicate to members the boundaries of behaviors that are acceptable. It is probably wise for the social worker to decide what format is most appropriate for the purpose of the group and the age of the child and to consistently use this arrangement. This provides a predictable environment for the child, one in which he/she can function flexibly without having to make adjustments to an ever-changing environment.

At the same time, it may be useful from time to time to purposefully change the format of the group, at least for a session. This often results in changes in the responses of the members, thus allowing for experimentation with new responses. An example of this occurred in an agency working with older latency children and adolescents.

The staff had learned from experience that occasional changes in length of sessions and format were very helpful to group interaction. The groups were expected to continue for two years. The usual pattern was for the group to meet one and one-half hours per week. It was expected that, every three months, one session was to be five hours long, and that every six months, a session would last seven or eight hours. These long meetings required and allowed for very different formats. At one such session, the members role-played some problems they were having at home and in school. They were unwilling to discuss their performance immediately after this activity. They complained of headaches and of not feeling well. They seemed to be too upset to continue with a discussion at that time. After eating dinner together in a very cordial, comfortable atmosphere, they began to discuss the situations played out in their earlier role-playing situations.

The format most often used with groups of children is one in which the children first participate in quiet activities for discussions, decision-making and planning for future sessions. This is followed by an active program that allows for more movement around the room. The rationale for this type of format is that once children have been involved together in very active ways, it is difficult for them to stop and relate to each other in a differing atmosphere.

An important consideration in determining the best format is awareness of what the children have been doing before they arrive at the group. Are they coming immediately from a classroom to another room in the same school? Or, are they walking six blocks to the meeting room? It is apparent that in the first instance, the children may need activity and freedom to move around, so a format that allows for this should be planned. In the second instance, the children may be ready to sit and discuss quietly.

Another dimension important in planning for the format is what is expected to happen to the child immediately after the session; that is, where is he/she going directly after the meeting ends? This can be of major concern, for example, if the group is meeting in the school and the child needs to return to the classroom.

The usual format of a children's group may be reversed, so that a more quiet activity occurs at the end, preparing the child for return to the classroom. Redl and Wineman (1957) illustrate and describe appropriate formats and activities to be used in very purposeful ways in their book *The Aggressive Child*. The thinking and planning delineated by them is equally useful and significant in working with all children.

The very nature of a group provides opportunities for children, after they become comfortable as a member, to explore and exert their autonomy as a member along with others both in a group or sub-group. They are attempting to change the structure as they perceive it. In the stage identified as "Stage II—Establishing My Place in the Group," the members are testing themselves with each other and with the worker. They are attempting to identify their position in the power structure of the group. As described earlier, it is during this stage that the worker begins to purposefully distribute a portion of the power to the group and its members. A structure still exists within which the group operates, but now members become a part of the power holders.

Member Roles

As noted by Levine (1979), younger children may be unable to assume as much power as older children because of their developmental level, but, at least on a temporary basis, they can be assigned some roles in the group by the worker where they can determine structure and act on their own decisions. When, for example, the worker asks a member to be in charge of distributing materials to the others, he/she is delegating an area of power to that child, which then is put into action by structure determined by the child. The worker remains the major power holder, distributing small assignments to the children that empowers them to structure a way of doing the tasks. Of course the worker or members may intervene in this process, creating a norm, (another type of structure) for how this task should be done in the future.

Meeting Room and the Immediate Environment

The meeting room is also a form of structure that is going to communicate to members the parameters of acceptable behavior. If children enter a meeting room to find the floor strewn with a large variety of toys, they are likely to pick up objects, look at them and throw them back on the floor. Even in an orderly room, placing large boxes of toys in the corner of the room (but still in sight of the children) is likely to be very stimulating. Two inexperienced group leaders decided to set up the room in this fashion for their first group session:

As was predictable, the first child or two entering the room went at once to the boxes, began to look and fling the materials over their shoulders and to move on to the next item. They were so stimulated they could not focus on any one item.

As noted in a previous chapter, depending on the particular problem and background of the child, this sort of stimulation might be helpful in getting members to act and communicate, or it may create chaos and cause the child to lose control.

Many other factors in the meeting room are going to set the scene for the members' behavior. For some children, locked cabinets in the room are almost intolerable (Slavson & Schiffer, 1975). This may be related to curiosity aggression or to previous life experiences. A child may be reacting because of what Redl and Wineman (1957, pp. 340–343) call an "individual antisepsis." They write that "sometimes a program may be 'good' on a variety of counts, but it so happens that a particular child is allergic to some of the ingredients it contains." Even norms or rules may contain some "individual antisepsis." This occurred in one group, as follows:

A number of children who had been seriously abused were to meet as a group. As always, the worker stated her rule that children could not leave the room during the session. Two of the members had been abused by being locked in one room together for their first seven years. For one of these twins, the worker's rule was totally intolerable, and thus the rules were modified for this group.

The size of the room, the type of chairs and other furnishings, (whether there are cushions on the floor or pictures on the wall), the sounds in the room and the immediate environment create part of the structure expected to affect the behaviors of the members. In a large room, the worker may have arranged a quilt on the floor with cushions carefully placed in a circle. This kind of scene would convey to most young children that this is a place to play games and also a cozy area where they can meet and talk together. Decorations, pictures and other objects may convey that this is a setting where children are welcome, that others have been here before and that people really like and care for children.

Rules and Norms

In almost all children's groups, the rules and norms that are identified by the worker and group are a very purposeful form of structure in the beginning sessions. The number and content of the rules may vary depending on the purpose, the problem of concern, agency rules and the beliefs of the practitioner(s). Sometimes rules of the agency or institution may automatically be upheld in the group. For instance, an organization may have a rule of not cursing in the building. The worker, because of wanting the children to experience the consequences of their behavior, identifies only a few broad rules of behavior. These rules do not include the "no cursing" rule of the agency. As a result, the group's children "try out" cursing and are confronted by other agency staff who overhear them in the halls. The worker, after becoming aware of this agency rule, supports it as a limit applicable to the group.

Tolerance for a variety of behaviors may differ greatly from one social worker to another. In order to establish meaningful limits, it is important for the worker to establish rules of behavior which are within his/her range of tolerance and are most fitting to the purpose of the group. More specific is an example of two differing workers, each with a group of older latency children. Members of both groups had been referred because of "delinquency prone behaviors." One worker had a great tolerance for "acting out" and hostile behavior. The means for behavior change for this worker was to establish one or two rules which were essential to the group's functioning, such as "the children are not to hurt each other or to destroy the building." This allows a great deal of space for member autonomy, thus allowing for positive or negative consequences to occur (within limits). The new learning is expected to produce change in behavior as a result of the consequences and the discussion and/or crisis that results.

Another worker, with much less tolerance of "acting out" behavior, may make a number of rules in an attempt to prevent the hostile, aggressive behavior from occurring. That worker may establish rules such as, "You must stay in your seat" and "You must raise your hand to be recognized before you speak." Obviously, children in this group are going to do less learning from experiencing the consequences.

Usually, the worker allows opportunities for the children, too, to state rules that they would like to have for "their" group. Caution must be used by the worker in allowing too many rules to be identified. Care must also be taken that the rules offered by the children are not in opposition to the purpose and method of the group.

The norm development that grows out of the experience of the group is the most meaningful and influential type for groups of children. An instance of this occurred in a group when a new social worker began meeting with a group after its former worker had left the agency.

During an early session, one member began to whisper into the ear of another member. There were immediate responses from the others about this being against the rules. It was clear that the members were asking the worker to take action to stop this behavior. To the worker, this seemed to be a rather strange rule with relatively few consequences. The members immediately began to explain that whispering caused a lot of anger and even fighting in the group, because they whispered about each other. It was clear that this was one of those norms that had developed as a result of the group's experience.

A major issue to keep in mind about rules or norms when working with children is how and by whom these are to be enforced. With very few exceptions, the expectation is that the worker is to enforce the rules. Care must be taken that any discussions include the rules and the consequences of violating them, so that the worker will administer the required response. Children are very aware and concerned about the fair application of rules to everyone.

For the latency age child, who is gradually experiencing and exploring the norms and values of others outside the family, the small group experience can be an especially meaningful one. As noted by Wilson and Ryland (1949, p. 40), "The organized group gradually replaces the parent as the source and testing ground of values and norms." In some ways, simply by making group rules the members "take away from their parents some measure of the regulatory function and delegate it to the group" (Wilson & Ryland, 1949, p. 40). In a sense, this movement away or testing becomes safer, because it becomes a group revolt.

It is also important to be aware of the role that the group workers play in norm development. They are the model for norms of the group. When Yalom (1985) described norm development, he stated that the worker cannot *not* influence the group norms. If the worker behaves in a particular way or purposefully decides not to behave, members will be affected, because the worker is seen in the beginning as having all the answers. The worker may also teach certain norms or rules through recognition and verbal or nonverbal responses to specific subject areas or member behaviors.

Over the life of the group, norms are continuing to develop, primarily as a result of learning and experiencing. Certainly in the latter stages of the group, members are very aware and in agreement about their code of behaviors.

The limits and structure inherent in activities and programs can also be very purposefully used by the worker. As identified by Wilson and Ryland (1949), even the materials used by the group place limitations on the members. For instance, a member who is finger painting is limited by the size of the paper. "The rules of the games and the accepted modes of accomplishing various other activities provide for some security through which they feel free to participate, and for others the irritations which accompany anything they are asked to do according to a form" (Wilson & Ryland, 1949, p. 167).

Some activities may define rules for the participants. Others may attract inactive, perhaps withdrawn, children into participation, as illustrated in the following:

One child who was very withdrawn and fearful of being rejected by others, played the board game "Sorry!" with a number of other group members and the worker. It was quickly realized that she was unable to slide the "game piece" and send another player back to "start." When this move was expected of her, she simply chose not to move at all or moved her "man" to the space behind the opponent. After participating in this game for several weeks, being repeatedly sent back to "start" and observing the positive and friendly competition between the others, she finally dared to send another member back. When she gained support from most of the players, her ability to take the expected risk was reinforced.

A special advantage of some activities is that "all participants can be involved in the action at the same time" (Middleman & Wood, 1990, p. 139). So, taking turns may not be required. This is especially helpful in working with very active latency age children. Often, if they are not continuously engaged in the activity, they create their own form of entertainment (perhaps in a harmful, hurtful manner). This is a program consideration which is described by Redl and Wineman (1957) and labeled as "frustration tolerance."

Games and activities with peers and others may allow latency age children to move through this developmental stage; first they are being controlled by their parents and other adults, then they search for other means of control, and finally they take more control of themselves. An intermediate step that children can take when beginning to assume responsibility for control of themselves can occur in a small group composed of peers who are interacting together.

Not only is there opportunity for peer influence, there are also group rules and norms. Even the games and activities, which are part of the group process, provide controls on behavior at least for a limited time.

One cannot play "tag," "dodge ball" or any other activity without rules. Restraints are imposed by the game itself and usually enforced by peers. So, the locus of control is moving from adults to peers, via the group and the rules of the game, and finally to the individuals themselves.

The use of structure, in the form of programming, can be a very potent means of implementing goal attainment for the members. The focus may be the individual child, the group as a whole or sometimes both the individual and the group concurrently.

Often, a game or activity will be suggested by the worker in order to intervene in the behavior of an individual. An example follows:

A child who was running wildly around the room and seemed to be almost totally out of control was asked to be the leader of "Crack the Whip." The worker took his hand and had the other children join hands and follow behind. In the beginning, the practitioner remained the first in line to help the child leader calm down and gain control of his behavior. The worker dropped out as this was accomplished, allowing the child to lead and bringing his behavior into the structure of the activity.

Games and activities can also act as a supportive structure, allowing members to "try out" a variety of roles. Working with a group of girls, a game such as "Mother, May I?" allows a very good opportunity for members to try on the role of being the authority and in control of others. So, a girl who is very shy and unsure of herself and her relationships with others is able to experience the use of control of members with their full support within the structure of the game. This activity may also be helpful to the other group members at the same time. The child who is playing the "it" role may have been the loner in the group, with very little attention or concern focused on her by others. This new experience may help her experiment more actively in relating to others, and they, in turn, may become more comfortable and accepting of her.

Sometimes, the worker may need to spontaneously identify and develop a structure to resolve an issue. A crisis in the group often precipitates this type of demand. One example is described below:

A group going to Disneyland stopped at its meeting room on the way out of town. The worker had the tickets for admissions and rides, but each child had additional spending money. Within a few minutes of arriving at the clubroom, one child stated that his money was missing. The worker, anxiously deciding what to do, stated some of her thoughts aloud. The members saw that the worker was attempting to deal with this issue. Before she could propose a way to solve the problem, a member suggested, "Let's turn the lights off and see if the money does not reappear." Some of the other members were skeptical of this solution, but the worker thought it was worth trying. They all stood around a large table with the lights off and their eyes closed. When the lights came on, the money had returned. A scene was set, or a structure was used, that allowed behavior to happen.

These parameters of behavior are especially useful in working with latency age children who are still very involved in fantasizing and believing in magic.

Other Forms of Structure

Rituals are another common form of structure used in groups (Middleman & Wood, 1990). These acts are often developed over time and relatively unique to a specific group. Rituals are most commonly used with children's groups for beginning and ending sessions. The use of these ceremonies is expected to help develop cohesion, through the promotion of group identity and a spirit of loyalty to the group. Often these rituals are also used to move toward accomplishment of members' goals. An example of this happened in a group of severely abused latency age children.

These children were latency age, but the level of functioning for some of them was at a lower level of development. The members named their club the "Charlie Brown Club." At the beginning and ending of each session, they repeated the same ritual: They held hands and recited together, "We are the Charlie Brown Club." Then, each member stated his/her name in turn. Finally they all jumped in the air with their arms raised over their heads and fell on the floor.

This ritual was a very simple one, partly developed by the worker and elaborated on by the members. Together, the children and members had selected a name for the group, after a great deal of deliberation. The use of the group name gave the children a positive identity; they were part of a special group of people who were friendly, acceptable to the world and genuinely liked and enjoyed by children and adults alike. This was in contrast to their real-life experience—that of having been severely abused by adults and of being foster children who were questioned and stigmatized by other children at school because their names were different from those of their guardians.

As a part of the ritual, the children were encouraged to state their names. This was to reinforce their identity and to help them overcome the shame they might associate with their names. Another purpose was to help them become acquainted and comfortable with each other. This part of the ritual was especially helpful for one child who had withdrawn from relationships and could (or would) not remember the name of anyone, including the co-leaders.

The last part of the ritual, jumping into the air and falling on the floor, was developed entirely by the children. It certainly served a purpose, too. There was a sense of fun and a way of relating, or "roughhousing together," that was comfortable for them. It also relieved the tension that accumulated as they participated in the first part of the ceremony.

Not only were rituals and symbols important to functioning in the group, they were also of potential use to the children outside the group. The symbols could be used to remind the children of their identity, even when they were not participating in a session.

Refreshments may also be used as a ritual or structure in many children's groups. This activity most often occurs at the beginning or end of a session, depending on the time of day. Food can provide an atmosphere conducive for children to sit quietly and eat. It also offers a time when the group members can discuss the happenings of the day and make plans for their next session. Even the type of refreshments and the manner of serving them can be a part of the structure. There may be a prescribed way in which cookies are passed to each child, for example.

For latency age children who are involved in fantasies and magic thinking, rituals in the group can be very enriching and provide additional areas for focus of attention. Also, rituals can provide a sense of sameness and predictability about what will happen in the session that day.

Another area of program that may become a form of rituals for some groups is the celebration of national holidays as special occasions. This type of activity may create a tradition and further develop cohesion, "which heighten(s) group identity and develops a spirit of loyalty to the group" (Middleman & Wood, 1990, p. 113).

Even rewards may help provide a way of structuring behavior in groups of children. These reinforcements may be used for a great variety of purposes. In a party-like atmosphere, they may be used to enhance members' motivation to compete with each other. They may also be used to encourage specific member behaviors, to help promote group cohesion and to reach any number of other purposes. The important consideration in the use of rewards is for the social workers to be very clear about their intent in using the reward or reinforcement. Not only is it important for the workers to know what the expected outcome is for the targeted member(s) or sub-group, but they need to be aware of possible outcomes for those members not targeted. For example, in using candy to reinforce or support specific behaviors desired, it is important to be very generous with the reward. If the focus of the reinforcement is two or three members, in order not to create factions in the group (thus continuing to promote cohesion), it is important that all of the members receive some candy, perhaps with those of concern receiving a bit more.

Rewards or other supports for children do not always have to be concrete objects. Very often in communicating with children, the social workers reinforce their behavior and/or attitudes and feelings both verbally and nonverbally:

A child who was fearful of rejection by other group members sat in a circle, allowing a very large space between herself and others. The worker very quietly pulled a chair up next to the child, as she said, "I would like to sit next to you today, if it's okay." The child nodded her head in agreement and others did not seem to notice.

Often the award is one's team being acclaimed as "the winners" or one's individual performance in drawing a work of art being placed on the wall. This special attention is often intended to support and reinforce appreciation of this person(s) as a unique, important and valued human being.

Often, the refreshments that are used as a part of most children's groups may be perceived by the members as their reward for participation in the group. It may be a way to convey that you are special and different from those boys and girls who are not members of the group. One of the purposes may be to promote feelings of group identity or cohesion. On an individual level, it may also be perceived by members as support (by an adult, the worker[s]).

In some instances, the use of refreshments may actually be used to feed children who arrive hungry to their meetings. This may result from the time of day of the session, or it may be because so many children are living in poverty:

One small group of six- and seven-year-old girls, on arriving at the settlement house for their meeting, went immediately to the agency pantry to choose refreshments from the stock of food supplies on hand. A large portion of their session was spent looking at pictures on the canned goods and talking about the contents and their likes and dislikes. It seemed important for these girls just to be able to touch the pictures on the cans and talk about food. After this continued for some time, they chose their refreshments for the group for that day. The worker remembers one memorable session, when the group selected "cream style corn" and peaches, an unusual combination.

A technique very akin to that of limit setting is that of setting the scene. The purpose of this behavior is to permit or allow behaviors to happen. This may be done in a variety of ways. In some instances, the worker may have arranged the room or special materials around the meeting area with the intent of "opening up" an area of discussion:

An example of this technique was used with a group of latency age children who had been removed from their homes. These children had been severely abused, placed in foster homes and finally put up for adoption. The practitioner thought that because of their limited experience in intact, nonviolent homes, that they probably had little conception of the roles that mothers and fathers played in families. To function appropriately in their soon-to-be adoptive families, they would need to have some notions about what might be expected of them in relation to other members. To promote this area of discussion, pictures of families doing things together were placed on the wall, and stories with pictures were placed on the tables. This encouraged members to look at, fantasize about and talk about what went on in these situations.

In summary, in working with latency age children, worker procedures involving limit setting or structuring are really techniques for empowering the child. Structures simply set parameters around an area of acceptable behavior and allow the child to make choices within those boundaries. This empowers the child to experiment, try a variety of behaviors and use self-determination within limits. Since children in this developmental stage are attempting to move from fantasy and magical thinking to viewing the world and the specific situations in a more realistic manner, a peer group experience that is empowering can enhance their individual growth. It is during this period that the child makes use of information gathered, integrated and retained, which finally becomes part of the person and his/her values and beliefs.

As evident in this chapter, the use of structures and settings provides major strategies for helping children grow and change. The next chapter describes the use of play and activities as a means of providing new means of coping, giving support and furnishing alternative behaviors.

Chapter 6

Play and Activity as Change Mechanisms

As indicated in previous chapters, the development of a mutual aid system and the use of structure and limits are crucial to the advancement of a group and for the children who participate. Another essential component vital throughout the life of a children's group is the use of play and activity.

TYPES OF PLAY AND ACTIVITY

It is useful to distinguish between structured and unstructured play. Unstructured play is a means of communicating and expressing oneself. It is used by all age groups, from infancy through aging, and is related to the individual's needs and to the people with whom he/she is in contact at a given time. The particular means of expression is likely to be related to the personality and group relationships of those participating. Garvey (1977) identified five criteria that define unstructured play: (1) it is pleasurable, or has a positive value for the player; (2) it is intrinsically motivated, with no external purpose or required action; (3) it is spontaneous and not compulsory; (4) it requires active participation by the player and; (5) it has a definite relationship to what is "not play" in the real world. This type of play occurs a great deal of the time in all kinds of situations and environments.

Qualities of Unstructured Play

Play is used by adults to learn about children in three ways (Garbarino, Stott et al., 1992). The first way is to assess the developmental level and competence of the child. This includes cognitive, social and physical development. The second use is to gain information about the child's inner life—to gain some idea of how the child feels. Third, play allows communication about stressful experiences.

"One of the most firmly established principles of psychology is that play is a process of development for a child" (Schaefer, 1980). Piaget (1969) points out that play allows children to mentally digest experiences and situations. Another expert in child development, Ginott (1961), indicated one way the child talks is with "toys as his words" (p. 27).

During preschool years and early childhood, children use pretend play to gain an increasing ability to manipulate fantasy and reality. Through play, children can deny ownership of distasteful or threatening ideas by using symbols. They can use an object to represent a person or can substitute one object for another. This allows them to transfer feelings from the real to the pretend or from the pretend to the real person or situation. In this manner, children can deal with anxiety-producing or sensitive material as if it were not their problem but rather belonged to someone else (Bateson, 1976).

Play also allows children to distance themselves from adults and the real world. In play and stories, they can reverse the roles that they play in reality. For example, if they are passive in "real life," they can "try on" the role of being active. For some children who have been abused, they can move from the role of the victim to being the perpetrator. "Through symbolic play, children can express ideas and feelings that would ordinarily be taboo" (Peller, 1978). They can express complexities, ambivalence and conflicting emotions (Mahler, Pine & Bergman, 1975). Adults talk about a trauma over and over again in an effort to deal with it, and sometimes children play out their traumatic experiences in a repetitive manner, too. Generally, the subjects, themes and plots in the play of latency age children are a combination of real-life experiences and fantasy.

Group play assists the child in developing skills for interacting with others outside the home (Bruner, Jolly & Sylva, 1976; Erikson, 1963; Herron & Sutton-Smith, 1971). The beginning skills for developing problem-solving abilities are acquired in the group play of children (White, 1966). Group interactions enhance the ability to think about what others are thinking and feeling. Children become more appreciative of differences, resolve conflicts and begin to understand the complementarity of roles (Piaget & Inhelder, 1969). In the group, some of the necessary work on identity takes place as members respond to each other, and each "tries on the differing roles for size." By adopting imaginary identities and by role-playing with peers, social development begins to take place.

Structured Play or Activities

Activities including games, races, storytelling, role-playing and dramas are all considered structured play. As these activities are used by the social worker to help members and groups attain their goals, they often are referred to as program. Program is identified by Middleman (1968) as developmental; that is, it is leading somewhere. The practitioner may use the limits and boundaries, or the roles intrinsic to the game, to help bring about change in the individual or group. This may be accomplished by the boundaries or roles required for participation in the game or activity. In the instance of playing checkers, there are rules of the game that provide limits of interaction and behavior. Or in an activity as free from rigid structures as role-playing, some limits and boundaries are utilized to identify and center the interaction that is expected to occur between the participants. Even a game of "tag" requires some limits and boundaries be set, sometimes by the children themselves before the game begins or as it progresses, to resolve the confusion and disagreements that may develop. Often, the children or worker stop the game after it is in progress to clarify or make a rule. Tag also includes the use of an "it" role, which involves the use of power, control and authority.

Program requires planning and implementing sequential activities intended to build one upon the other, in order to move members and/or the group toward specific goals or purposes. A worker may have a goal in mind such as beginning to develop a group from an aggregate of individuals. He/she might first plan to have an introductory exercise, followed by some discussion and orientation to the group, then games already familiar to the children, followed by refreshments. These activities are grouped together in a playful manner in order to move toward the longer-term goal of becoming a group.

All of this range of program, levels of communicating and interacting are primary tools used by social workers in working with groups of children. The structured and unstructured play may not be evident in observing a group in interaction, however, it is useful for the practitioner to be aware of some of the characteristics and uses of each type.

Play or Activity as a Tool

In latency, children turn to more structured activities (such as games) that allow them to practice living within a set of specific rules. Games and other structured activities provide a useful tool for the social worker to employ in assisting the child to develop and to change behaviors when necessary. As identified by Middleman and Wood (1990), the major purposes for the use of activities are: helping the isolated, silent and withdrawn individual; helping people "learn the rules of the game"; and helping members move beyond where they are; that is, making new discoveries and developing creativity.

By involvement in games and other structured activities, many of the child's social and developmental needs are met with relatively little worker involvement. Lieberman (1979, p. 291) indicated that "games governed by rules are an important part of life during latency. The rules provide the external controls that were previously imposed by parents, help develop skills and provide an outlet for competitive strivings." Games often encourage laughing and joking, which may relieve anxiety and facilitate participation. There are opportunities for following rules, taking turns, giving feedback and learning to both win and lose. "Games provide an opportunity for the child to learn the consequences of his actions without having to suffer them" (Cartledge & Milburn, 1981, p. 100). Within the context of a game, mistakes and exposure of ignorance are more tolerated.

In games, control is lodged in the rules rather than with the practitioner. In observing a group of children playing baseball on a vacant lot or playground, it is clear that no adults are needed or, in most cases, wanted. The use of rules as they are interpreted and modified in that group are sufficient to manage the behaviors of the group and the members. Within the games or activities, there are also roles that shift control from one participant to another. This occurs in a game of "tag," for example, when the person who is "it" may play an important role in the control of others and their behavior. Participation with other children in a structured activity shifts control from parent, teachers and workers to the game itself.

Activities other than games are also very useful in assessing the difficulties that children may experience as well as in providing a tool to help children change by presenting them with alternative behavior or ideas. Arts, crafts, drawing, coloring, playing with puppets, taking photographs of members and using a tape recorder or video camera are all useful as tools to help members and groups accomplish their goals. The use of "play-like," role-playing or drama is often very functional in helping children modify or expand their thinking and feelings. Most children move easily into this type of activity. With some, it is essential to move gradually and allow them to feel safe in participating at each step (Fatout, 1993).

One way to move toward role playing in the group may be to ask members what they might do or say in a particular situation. An example of this occurred when one of the members related his experience:

The member, who was living in a foster home, said he was asked by a schoolmate about whether he was living with his parents. He had responded, "It's nothin' to you," but obviously was not happy with his response or the reaction of the other boy. However, since others in the group were in foster homes too, there were expressions of understanding and some sharing of similar experiences. Members were asked to think about how they had answered similar questions in the past and what would be a "good" way to respond. From there, they tried a variety of possible responses. The next step was to have two children role play and talk about how they felt when answering in a particular way, and about how the receiver would feel hearing this response.

For most children, gradual movement into role-playing does not feel like risk taking as it would if they were thrown into an activity too quickly.

In order to encourage children to participate in this type of activity, any of the props associated with pretending can be utilized. This helps the children distance themselves and at least momentarily deny the reality of their response to the situation, thus minimizing risk taking. Many types of physical settings and materials may set the scene for the children moving into role-playing or drama as means of resolving issues or problems. Sometimes, meeting in a room where there is a stage or something that could become a pretend stage (wooden boxes or children's tables) stimulates one or two children, later joined by others, to mime songs or act. Other materials that are useful are paper sacks or other masks placed over the head to distance the real person from the situations being played out.

Old clothes can be a resource that provides even more potential for experiencing a variety of roles with multiple dimensions. Children love to try on men's or women's clothing and look at themselves and pretend. They also like to elicit responses from peers, the social worker and sometimes even from the general public (if they go out onto the street). In order to reduce the risk taking, the use of a "costume" (the old clothes) may be a part of a role-playing activity. Focusing in this way makes the clothes an essential part of creating an activity for pretend that allows children to freely express a variety of behaviors and feelings without really exposing themselves. At the same time, as the "costume" is selected for playing the role, there are opportunities to try many clothing options, view oneself in a mirror and receive responses from peers and the worker.

Spontaneous Action Events

Another type of activity that occurs in groups is one that is identified here as spontaneous action events. These events grow out of the history of the group and the members, their needs and the processes that have occurred to this time. They are similar to "critical incidence" written about in working with adult groups, but because children often express their feelings by both actions and words, these events now take on the appearance of activity or program.

These experiences result in shared social experiences for the members and the group. They are unplanned by the practitioner and the group. Often, it is this type of experience that seems most meaningful in moving the group and its members toward goals. Opportunities for interactions of this type arise often and can be utilized by the worker to create growth.

An example of this happened in a group of older latency age boys who were angry at their worker. During the session, the boys had been unable to reach major decisions about a trip they were planning. The worker indicated that they could not go on the trip until the planning had been completed. They vented their frustrations and anger upon the worker. It was time to leave the clubroom and decisions had not been made. The worker said it was time for him to take the boys home in the agency van.

As the worker prepared to close and lock the rooms, the boys began to actively express their feelings. The boys' behaviors ranged from turning lights on as the worker turned them off and rolling billiard balls down the steps toward the glass doors to balancing themselves on a five-inch ledge on the second-floor stairwell. The final expression of anger was displayed as the boys sat in the car awaiting the worker's arrival. They blew the horn and locked the van doors. As the practitioner used the key to unlock the door, a boy would immediately press the lock button. Finally, the worker signaled, by arms extended and palms up, that he gave up.

As the worker entered the van, the members were extremely quiet. He said, "I don't understand why you are having such difficulty in making a decision this time. You have done it before." The worker drove from the parking lot. There was silence for almost two blocks until one of the members asked the worker to park so they could make their plans. Now they were able to do this.

Out of the group members' anger at the worker, because they felt he had usurped some of their power and control, came a great deal of action and almost no verbalizing about feelings. In this instance, a great deal of unplanned behavior and activity happened that could be utilized by the worker to set limits and express belief in their abilities, allowing them to resolve the conflict and move on.

In another group, a trip was made from the members' relatively small community to a Jewish community center in Los Angeles to swim in the pool. One member, who was starting to feel more confident about herself, had just begun to reach out to others in her neighborhood and to test how accepted she was by them. She dared to ask one of the men in the pool if he would help her learn to swim, which he did. This was an exceedingly daring thing for this girl to do, the man was from a different economic and ethnic group, in an unknown and unfamiliar neighborhood. To her great surprise, she found that he accepted her and was willing to give her the assistance she requested. She enthusiastically told the others of her experience on the ride home.

In these two instances, the children went beyond talking to using patterns of behavior that communicated needs, issues and attempts at problem-solving. This is the type of activity that is not planned by anyone and has no obvious rules. It is activity of this variety that is the most real and demanding of the practitioner. Often, the external conduct of a group simply cannot be ignored; it requires a response or attempts to limit it. In order to understand what the surface behaviors are communicating, it is essential to understand the underlying dynamics of the actions that are occurring. Simply limiting the behavior often does not resolve the underlying issues that are being expressed. Sometimes, if the worker successfully quells the current activity, similar acts appear at a later time in the group and often continue from time to time until the issue is resolved. An example of this process was evident in the behavior of a group of older latency age girls described as follows:

Once, while riding in the agency van, the members began to make hand signals and giggle. The practitioner watched and wondered what the girls were doing, as they only laughed and tussled with each other more. The behavior stopped that session but reappeared from time to time. The worker was bewildered about the hand gestures, having no idea what they meant. As she attempted to explore this by asking questions, the members only became more excited and disorderly. Their behavior seemed to be serving at least two purposes: They were trying to convey a concern and also were getting some enjoyment from having a secret that excluded the worker. This latter was most appropriate for their age.

Finally, before the behavior began at another session, the worker indicated that she really did want to help them with whatever they were attempting to tell her. After some guessing, she found that it had to do with boy/girl relationships. They proceeded from this topic to talk about kissing boys from differing racial and ethnic backgrounds.

The worker thought that they had worked through the issue as they sat in the van before entering the meeting room. However, when they arrived, they began to dance closely together with very slow music, turning to look at the practitioner quite often. The worker had never seen this behavior before and knew that it was significant. They had danced together often but never like this. After bringing the group together and discussing the members' concerns, it was clear that the girls were curious about boys' bodies and how they functioned.

As was evident in this situation, the members continued to express, through their behaviors, a need that they were unable or unwilling to verbalize. They wanted to know more about the physiology of the male. They were tenacious about conveying their message and need and were not going to give up until it was successfully worked through. The examples described demonstrate this combination of talking and doing that can be purposefully used to achieve member and group goals.

This type of activity requires the practitioner to have a very good understanding of the underlying dynamics of the members' behaviors in the situation. Most social workers find the use of this type of spontaneous action event to be very challenging, stimulating and also very demanding. The worker must be looking, listening and thinking continually to decode the messages that groups, sub-groups or members are attempting to send. Some tension is relieved by the knowledge that if the worker does not receive the message the first time, it will probably be repeated again and again.

FITTING ACTIVITIES TO THE PROBLEMS/NEEDS

Generally, activities can make a contribution to the members' and group's development. Northen (1988, pp. 78-79) identified the uses for activity as follows: (1) to assist the social worker in assessing the members and/or group; (2) to reduce stress, give pleasure and allow for creativity; (3) to facilitate communication of feelings, ideas and experiences; (4) to stimulate reflective and problem-solving discussions; (5) to develop relationships between members and cohesion in the group; (6) to provide opportunities for giving to others; (7) to develop basic skills; (8) to cultivate competence in making and implementing decisions; and (9) to use and/or change the environment. A primary concern in working with the group is to help members develop to their maximum ability. As noted by Northen (1988, p. 96), "Competence can be achieved by people only to the extent that there are opportunities to develop it."

Social workers with groups have developed broad and rich knowledge of the use of activities as therapeutic tools (Garvin, 1987; Konopka, 1983; Middleman, 1968; Middleman & Wood, 1990; Northen, 1988; Vinter, 1986a; Whittaker, 1986; Wilson & Ryland, 1949). Almost any activity can be used for this purpose. In writing of activity, which she refers to as program, Middleman (1968, p. 65) states, "The concept of program employed here is a dynamic one demanding much creativity, flexibility, and adaption of the given activity to the particular needs of the group and its individual members at any given moment in time." It is a tool applied differentially to suit the occasion, and sometimes as it is applied, it also changes as the group, members and worker modify it to fit their needs and goals.

Often, names of activities can be altered by the social worker to fit the needs and the stage of the group and to make them more appealing to the participants. For example, in working with a group of young latency age boys, the worker may go beyond simply suggesting a game of tag.

To create excitement, he/she may call the activity "Power Rangers and bad guys."

Another way of altering activities may be to change roles or names of roles within that game; that is, by placing a specific child within a special role because of his/her special need. A child who is withdrawn and has low status in the group may be placed in a highly visible position in the activity. A game such as "Follow the Leader" allows the worker to select this child to lead the others, or in "Simon Says," allows the leader to control the whole group. Once, a beautician had offered to come to a session to speak to a group of girls. Adrianne, one of the members, often came to group dirty and not very well groomed. All the girls wanted to be "models." It was finally decided that Adrianne could be the very first "model" for that session.

There are many opportunities within games and other activities to alter names, roles, the equipment and space needed to create a better fit with the needs of the members and the group as a whole. In order to accomplish this, the social worker must have individualized each member and his/her needs. Sometimes, it is not possible to plan for these changes in advance; the practitioner must be creative and alert to the opportunities that may arise within the situation. Because the children participate along with the worker in determining the content of a session, many activities are unplanned until the decision is made in the group session.

Over the latency period, there is a great deal of physical and mental development in the child that may result in the use of activities that are different from the beginning to the ending of this stage (see Chapter 2). Often in early latency, children cannot bear to lose and always want to be first and to change rules to suit themselves. As children mature during this developmental stage, they are likely to insist on rules and fairness. At this time, skills usually become more important than winning the game. At the beginning of this period, play can be described as autonomous, as the child does handstands, skates, climbs and rides a bicycle. As the child gets older, he/she uses peers to measure personal worth and level of skill. It is skill development that often binds children together around play and special interests that they may develop (Cohen, 1972).

Young latency age children are likely to discharge tension by repetitious movements, so it is useful to plan relays or activities that promote skipping, hopping, running or rope jumping accompanied by chants that help keep the cadence. In writing of games, Flavell (1985, p. 74) states, "These provide collective rules that enable the child to learn the ways and values of other children." Over time, children play out social roles together and thus learn society's versions of reality and establish their own identity.

Planning for Activities with Children

Generally, it is expected that the social worker is primarily involved in helping the group select and use activities. With latency age children, the role of the practitioner includes many specific tasks. Often, the worker must select an activity, plan, initiate, teach, support, modify and enrich the group's experience.

With knowledge of what children are developmentally expected to do, the practitioner must focus more on the activity that he/she plans to use with them. Vinter (1974a) identified a formulation for analyzing activities that is helpful in selecting programs that will fit with specific groups composed of members with specific skills, abilities and developmental levels. He identified a number of dimensions that are important to think about as one matches an activity to the group and its members.

These areas to be assessed are as follows:

- *What behaviors are required to participate?* The range of rules and expected conduct of participants are important to consider for children. Young latency age children can participate in large body movement activities. As the children begin to mature, more refined controlled muscle movement is possible.

- *Where is control located?* Control may be located in a person outside the group, such as a person acting as an umpire in a baseball game; in the rules of the game, as enforced by the participants; or in a specific role in the group, for example, Simon, in "Simon Says."

- *How much physical movement is required or permitted?* The focus is on assessing the broad physical boundaries and the use of whole body muscles as compared to small physical space and refined muscle control.

- *What is the minimum level of ability required to participate?* It is important that every child in the group is able to participate at a level that is acceptable to the group. In a group where the skill level of all the members is low, any child who can participate at a minimum rate would be acceptable. If the average skill level of the members is high, then a child who performs at a very low level would not be acceptable.

- *What are the opportunities for members' interaction within the activity?* Within most activities for children, there is an abundance of opportunities for interaction. This is necessary because of the needs of children and their occasional inability to control behavior. In many games, there are both formal and informal occasions to interact. An example of this is in playing "Red Rover." There are prescribed statements that each team says to the other, and then there is running, chasing and catching each other that allows for a broad range of types of verbal and nonverbal interaction for everyone.

- *What rewards are available to participants?* It is important to be aware of how many rewards are available to the members as they participate in the activity. All activities provide some opportunity for rewards, such as through winning, praise for the output object, releasing tension and improving skills. In working with children, especially with young latency age in the beginning stages, it is important to create cohesiveness rather than distance between the members. As a result, activities in which there are opportunities for a wide distribution of rewards will be important to help members react positively to each other rather than jealously and competitively. In contrast, with older latency age children there may be real value in having a greater scarcity of rewards. Since children in this developmental stage are more interested in skill and competition, demonstration and rewarding of skills may be highly valued. In this latter situation, the social worker would be more concerned about providing a variety of activities where each member has the opportunity to receive some reward. Obviously, many groups may be in transition between these two extremes and require a combination of types of rewards.

As the practitioner attempts to match activities with the group and its members, there are some individual variables that must be taken into account, such as the level of skill the children possess, the motivation the children have to participate in the activity and the on-tap control of each child.

Special Uses for Activities

Although the focus for Redl and Wineman (1957) was working with aggressive children, many of their guidelines and suggestions are also very applicable to planning and working with children during the latency period. If the children are excited, anxious and running around hitting each other (especially as special holidays approach), there may be a pileup of impulsive energy that is being discharged by this reckless disorganized behavior. The worker, by recognizing the underlying cause of this behavior, may provide an activity that allows for discharge within the structure of organized play, a game or other forms of program.

Another concern in planning activities for children is their level of frustration tolerance. Many children, if faced with the need to wait a turn to participate in a game such as "Pin the Tail on the Donkey" create their own "program" during the wait. They may, for example, begin their own game by chasing and hitting each other until it is their turn. It is important for the practitioner to be aware of, and plan for, the frustration threshold of the child in the group with the lowest level of frustration tolerance.

Most children feel threatened by new situations that are unfamiliar to them. In these cases it is important to introduce new activities gradually, as in the following example:

A group of latency age boys from the inner city of a metropolitan area were planning to go to an agency-owned cabin in the woods and had to be prepared over time for this new experience. One step in this preparation was to take the boys on a day-long trip to a heavily wooded park, allowing them to become acquainted with this type of area and to find activities and resources that were fun to do in this new setting.

Another way to help children cope with new, unfamiliar activities is to cultivate interests by setting the scene for contagion to occur. One child may bring a yoyo to the group; others may not be familiar with how to use it, but as they observe the tricks and skill necessary, they all want to try playing with it. Or, the worker may have a special interest such as flying a kite. As the children arrive for the group, the worker is flying a kite. After observing and perhaps holding the string on the practitioner's kite, they all want to try it. In planning the session, the worker prepared for this response by bringing kites for the children to use.

The Practitioner's Role in Activities

A relatively unique characteristic of working with groups is that the practitioner often participates in the activities. The purpose of this is not for the worker's own entertainment, but rather for a variety of other reasons. The worker, for example, may enjoy the activity and can model appropriate ways of displaying this. It is also important to some of the older latency aged children that the worker have fun in being with and participating with them. A situation like this occurred after a trip to an amusement park. One of the girls seemed rather dejected and said to the worker, "But you didn't have any fun." The practitioner was shocked that the girl had observed this fact and that she cared enough to comment. The child, along with the others, had been running from one ride to another as fast as she could. The worker had been to this same park many times with other groups and was feeling rather bored at being there again. She felt that it did not make a difference how she behaved, because the children were so busy that they would not notice. She found, to her great surprise, that it did make a difference and that her participation and enjoyment were important to the girls.

Often as the worker participates, there are occasions to demonstrate his/her vulnerability in terms of skills or knowledge. This offers opportunities for members of the group to demonstrate their superior skills, thus allowing the power of the worker to be distributed among the members.

Children are often much more skilled in drawing than the worker. This fact becomes obvious to the children and allows the worker to model behavior of a person who may not be as skilled as some of them. It lets them know that it is alright not to be the best at everything.

Another important reason for the worker to participate with the children is that it often helps to divert some of his/her attention from what they are doing. In drawing pictures or working with modeling clay or "Play doh," the worker often participates, allowing the children more occasions to express themselves freely without feeling that they are being supervised by the worker.

As the practitioner participates, his/her end product of the activity is not the important outcome. As indicated above, there are many other purposes that are related to helping the members accomplish their goals. Often, the worker may begin to participate and abandon his/her project to assist the children who may need help in accomplishing theirs. The worker may not become directly involved at all with some activities but rather remain ready to assist the children as required. Children may be hindered in some of their very active games by the direct participation of the worker.

Probably the best way for workers to assess whether their participation is useful for the group and its members is to ask themselves the purpose for participating. The answer to that question should alert them as to whether it is their needs being met or those of the children.

Worker skills in facilitating activities. Social workers, in the literature, have described some specific ways to involve children in activities (Garvin, 1981; Gitterman & Shulman, 1986; Henry, 1992; Levine, 1979; Northen, 1988). There are some generally accepted beliefs about factors that are important in conducting activities with children (Redl & Wineman, 1957; Trieschmann, Whittaker & Brendtro, 1969). Many of these have already been discussed. Other areas that are considered important are as follows:

1. One key factor in initiating a successful activity is using one's own enthusiasm. If a worker is not expecting an activity to be fun, it probably will not be.
2. It is also important to end games and some activities when things are going well and children are enjoying themselves. (The exception is activity that involves the production of an end product.) When these same programs are suggested in the future, the children will remember how much they enjoyed them in the past.
3. It is often important not to place too much emphasis on the finished product. The creativity and imagination utilized in making it may be more important.
4. It is important to be ready to switch activities in mid-stream if they are not going well. This probably means that the social worker needs to come to the group with many ideas for other games or activities that could be substituted.
5. Often, the activity can be started just by beginning. The whole group does not always need to be called together to begin. The worker may involve a few members in the beginning, and then others will join in as they become aware of the opportunity to participate.

During program, the practitioner must often be focused on individual participants as well as the group as a whole. Sometimes, the purpose of this is to create a desire to participate and motivate others to become more involved. Other times, it may be to control and inhibit behaviors of those who may be overinvolved or overstimulated. In individualizing the group members, the practitioner may be able to intervene during an activity when a child needs special help. Often, support can be given to a child during a craft project by simply making a comment, asking a question or in some way paying attention to what the child is doing. This recognizes that the child is there and viewed as important by the worker. Support can become more evident if the worker pulls a chair over and sits down next to the child or even reaches over to help the child find a crayon or cut part of a craft object. This can also provide the support that assists the child to get over a frustrating hurdle that he/she has been facing. Not only does that make the child feel supported, it may also help that child to gain status in the group.

The worker may also limit behavior of members in a variety of ways as an activity continues. In some situations, "planned ignoring" (Redl & Wineman, 1957, p. 400) can be used. This is useful when the practitioner sees a behavior that has the potential of being disruptive to the activity and others in the group. If the practitioner assesses that the behavior will stop of its own accord or of its own exhaustion, it can be ignored.

The next step in controlling a member's behavior may be to signal to the disruptive member that this behavior is not acceptable. This signal may be shaking the head, wagging the finger or a number of other universally understood gestures. If the worker is close enough to the child who is beginning to lose control, a touch on the shoulder or arm may have a calming influence.

A child involved in an activity may misinterpret something within the situation that has just occurred. An example of this happened in a group of young girls who were playing a circle game where the girl who is "it" steps in front of another child, and the latter one then becomes "it." The child who was "it" had just turned her ankle and was making a series of faces that others saw as humorous. So as "it" stepped in front of the girl, some of the others were laughing hysterically. The new "it" was very shy and unsure of herself, and thought they were laughing at her. She appeared ready to withdraw from the game. The worker intervened by interpreting to the child what had occurred that she had not seen.

In this case, the worker's interpretation was used to support the child's participation. It is often used to de-escalate behavior, such as a child reacting aggressively when he/she thinks that someone in the game has been too aggressive. Interpreting or limiting behavior would be useful in this situation.

Once in a while, it may become necessary to remove a child from a conflict situation. Ordinarily, this is only done as a last resort, when a situation cannot be worked through in any other way.

In some cases, in order to limit and control behavior, it may be necessary to abandon the current activity and substitute a more suitable one that is more appropriately timed to the mood, attitude and readiness of the group.

As is evident in this chapter, play and activity are very important tools for working with groups of latency aged children. The social work practitioner must develop knowledge and skills in order to use these instruments to assist the child in learning to cooperate with others, to negotiate conflicts and to take others into account. It is not the game, activity or product that is important but rather the skills developed in learning to respect each other and to work out solutions to problems in a nonviolent manner.

Development of the child is dependent on play, the use of imagination in activities and learning the rules from others in games that at a later time will be used to help them live in an adult world. Without this arena of latency age group participation, many lessons needed for living in society might be missed and left unlearned by children as they grow into adulthood.

Several previous chapters have focused on specific elements of working with children's groups. It is also important for the practitioner to be aware of a broader picture focused on the many conditions and processes that occur and change over time. This is the content of the upcoming chapter.

Chapter 7

Using the Group Process

By using a variety of methods and procedures, the social worker attempts to help the group and the members move toward their goals. Strategies that are especially important in working with children are developing and establishing a mutual aid system (to the degree that the children are able), using limits and structures and utilizing play and activities. These strategies are major tools for helping bring about change in children's groups. As these strategies are used, there are also changing conditions or dynamics in the group. These are called processes.

PROCESS AS A CONCEPT

Process, as used in group work literature, is change that takes place in group conditions. Change can either be described by selecting a group structure and examining how it changes over time or as it occurs moment to moment in interactions between the members (Garvin, 1987). Both of these means of focusing on change within the group are significant in working with children, because the social worker has more direct influence on the group process in working with children than would generally be true in working with adult groups and has the opportunity to guide this process toward accomplishment of goals.

The final outcomes in the group may be viewed as a developmental sequence that gradually moves from one level of social organization to another. This way of conceptualizing group outcomes is especially appropriate for children's groups because of the concurrent organizational development of both the group and the member. Not only is there change in the group as an entity, but because of the physical, psychological and social growth of the members, both within and outside the group, this process is further evolved and more vital.

Role of the Practitioner

It is the task of the social worker to facilitate the process in such a way that the group becomes the prime influence on the behavior of its members as they mature and develop sufficiently to change. As the practitioner is aware of the process and understands its meaning, it is possible, when necessary, to modify or redirect the members' interactions to move toward attainment of individual and/or group goals. This involves motivating and assisting members by both supporting and challenging them. In situations when it is recognized by the worker and members that a structure must be changed, some form of intervention may be required. The practitioner's task in working with children is to help them progress as much as they are able toward the conditions described by Middleman and Wood (1990, p. 92). These authors state, "As we see it, social workers do not run groups. They help groups to organize, develop, and run themselves. They help the participants to develop a system of mutual aid."

CHANGES IN STRUCTURE AS PROCESS

One way of viewing process in groups, as noted above, is to look at the changes in structure that have occurred over time. There is not always agreement between authors about those dimensions identified as structure. Henry (1992) differentiates between the external and internal structure of the group. The external structures are time, space and size, which have already been addressed in a previous chapter. Internal structures, according to Henry, are the conditions that may be expected to change as the group develops: roles, cohesion, communication, decision-making, norms, values, group culture, group control and influence. Garvin (1981, p. 96) basically identifies the same group structures, but he arranges or categorizes them in the following conditions: communication, sociometric, power, leadership and role.

Group Dimensions

Probably the most detailed listing of structures are those that Levine (1979, pp. 86–87) refers to as "group dimensions." By using his listing of structures, it is possible to describe the expected process in children's groups over time in terms of stages.

Differentiation of members from each other in the first stage of the group is usually minimal. Potential members of the group enter as a conglomerate of individuals who flock together, each somewhat fearful of being rejected by the others or by the practitioner. In the beginning, individuals may be reluctant to be noticed as different in any way.

With some testing of the acceptance of others in the group, a few members may dare to expose some of their more unique characteristics and behaviors to the social worker and thus to the other members. This may occur rather gradually with young latency age children. Often with older latency children, this testing of the worker and the environment may transpire by the use of sub-groups that begin to form. In this stage, "Establishing My Place in the Group," the primary differentiation confirmed is that of the members from the practitioner.

It is in the third group stage, "Working on My Goals and Those of Other Members," when the most differentiation between members becomes evident. As workers recognize and identify specific needs and problems of individuals, they may begin to focus on an individual to work on an issue of concern. This act of the practitioner helps the children become more aware of themselves as individuals, differing in some ways from the others and having problems/needs unique to themselves. This process coincides with the developmental growth of older latency children as they begin to compare themselves to peers as a way of measuring themselves in knowledge and skills. Young latency age children may remain relatively undifferentiated in this stage.

In the last group stage, "We Prepare Ourselves and End the Group," the primary area of differentiation for the young latency child is that of the member from the practitioner. If the children are attending school together, there may still be strong feelings of being closely connected with other members. This may promote less feelings of differentiation, at least in some areas of functioning. As the memory of the group experience fades and the children mature, acceptance of differences of themselves and others becomes more acceptable. For the older latency child who has developed some greater approval of self and other, the termination of the group provides differentiation from members of the group.

Affective polarities refer to the valence of emotions. There are expected to be changes in this structure that contribute to the therapeutic benefits of the group. In the first group stage, both the younger and older latency children are involved with feelings of trust versus mistrust. In the second group stage, the children are concerned with acceptance versus rejection. It is during the third group stage that many of the young latency children are still focused on acceptance. Some of the older latency children have moved to autonomy versus intimacy. In the last stage for children, the emotional response is likely to be satisfaction versus dissatisfaction.

Behavior features are closely tied to the affective dimensions. Typical behaviors for the children during the "Getting Acquainted" stage are approach versus avoidance actions. For the children, the target of this behavior is likely to be the social worker and the environment. They are exploring the resources and the environment for future use. The stage, "Establishing My Place in the Group," involves fighting and flocking by some of the older latency children. As they begin to explore each other, sub-groupings often occur related to the activity. The younger children are still likely attempting to establish themselves primarily with the practitioner, with less concern evident in relation to each other.

As the group moves into the third stage, when the focus is on accomplishing goals, there is a greater emergence of affective behavior and concern for each other, both with older and younger latency age children. The nature of the stage, often with the practitioner's active participation in problem-solving, helps to produce understanding of the problems of each member, so that more affective ties are established. During the termination stage, the children may regress, complain and deny that the group is ending. A few may be able to express satisfaction in goals that they have achieved.

Source of gratification is the dimension that may be the most related to the maturity of the latency age group. For most young latency children, the social worker is likely to be the greatest source of gratification throughout the group experience. By the third stage, "Working on My Goals and Those of Other Members," some of the younger children will now be gaining a great deal of pleasure and satisfaction from other members as well as from the practitioner.

For the older children, the worker is the primary source of gratification in the beginning. As they progress through the second stage, the source of satisfaction and enjoyment for most of them will be both the practitioner and other members. At the time of termination, the source of gratification for the older children is likely to be themselves and other members.

Relational issues are the same for both older and younger latency age children in the beginning. The children generally are in conflict about making contact with others or remaining isolated. The younger children will probably move through the second, and perhaps the third and fourth stages, primarily focused on relationships with the social worker. For some of the younger children, more focus may be placed on other members during the working stage.

For older latency children, much more focus is placed on the other members as well as the worker by the second stage. Relationships, both with members and the worker, continue to be the nucleus of interest up until the time of termination. It is at this time that bonds may be loosened, or there may be attempts to carry over relationships into the world outside the group.

Self/other concept in the beginning is the same for older and younger latency age children. They are concerned about how much they have in common with or are different from the other members. The younger latency children will be concerned about this issue until the third stage, when the practitioner begins to more clearly individualize the members and helps them move toward their goals. In this process, the others begin to see, understand and differentiate differences among themselves. As they are also involved in helping members attain their goals, these differences are more likely to become acceptable to them. So by termination, most of the children continue to recognize commonalities but are also beginning to accept the differences between self and others.

Because of maturity, the older children may begin to be more comfortable with the uniqueness of themselves and others by the end of the second stage of group development. This area of concern may be very important as they test themselves against others in terms of their abilities and skills. By the third group stage, they may remain competitive but are usually accepting of individual characteristics of themselves and others. At the time of termination, members will probably be able to separate self and others with greater clarity.

Power relationships are an important dimension of the group to analyze and assess. In the beginning for latency age groups, power is vested in the practitioner. For younger children, this basically continues until termination. In the third stage, "Working on My Goals and Those of Other Members," for short periods of time the children may take on more power as it is assigned or delegated by the worker. Having completed the task or assignment, the child generally moves back into a relatively powerless relationship with the other members. There is likely to be competition among the members to hold some power, even for a short time. During this group stage, there is some slight sharing of power among the members, but power is clearly vested in the social worker.

The older latency children also delegate most of the power to the worker. They may seek more power for themselves not as a group to share the power among the members, but rather as individuals in competition with each other. In the latter part of the third stage, there may be some evidence that for short periods of time the members may take the power from the worker and share it among themselves. It is this type of process that begins to develop the potential for the development of a mutual aid system described previously. As the group is terminated, any power that has been gained by the individuals is relinquished.

Conflict is very much a part of any group. Generally in the initial stage, conflict is relatively minimal. As the members establish their place in the group, more member-to-member conflict emerges. This may continue to escalate with latency children as they seek to gain favor with the practitioner. The worker, in the process of focusing on members and group goals, may defuse this process by centering attention on working together to assist each other in making desired changes. As noted earlier, the older latency age children have a greater capacity to focus on others and their problems than do the younger children, but beginning strides can be made by both groups in this area.

Cohesion is the bond or affective ties that hold the group together. The development of this relationship between members can be identified when they begin to recognize that others are absent from the group on a certain day. The importance of the group to its members is also indicated when they start arriving early for their sessions.

In viewing cohesion as a structure of children's groups, it is very related to the ages of the individuals involved. The younger latency children have primary ties to the practitioner throughout the life of the group. Certainly, they may have cultivated a best friend in the group, but the group members as a whole will probably remain fragmented and be dependent on the worker to hold them together as a unit. The older latency age children enter the group with primary ties to the worker; this continues during the first two stages. By the time they focus on their goals in the third stage, they may have begun to develop ties to each other so that group bonds are deepened.

Controls in the beginning are vested in the worker. Younger children allow the controls to remain primarily with the worker throughout the life of the group. Generally, the practitioner delegates control to a member or sub-group for a short period of time to accomplish a very specific task. Usually, the worker takes care to give every child opportunities to experience being responsible for some amount of control, even if it is no more than passing out the napkins for refreshments. In this way, there are opportunities for the young children to experience control for short periods of time.

Children generally will test to assure themselves that the worker is in control. The testing process may give the appearance that the members are seeking control, but generally the children want to assure themselves that the worker is in control and that they will be protected even from their own out-of-control behavior. An example of this is a child who runs into the street in a very teasing manner, waiting for the adult to limit this behavior. The child may feel especially close to the worker after he/she has been pulled back upon the sidewalk and reminded of the danger.

Older latency age children, who have had more experience with control even for short periods of time, may be ready to take on more regulation of themselves and the group as a whole. Readiness to take on control of the group, however, is partly dependent on the maturation level of the members. Taking control "results in some loss or modification of self, as the individual identifies with the group and its direction of movement" (Henry, 1992, p. 15). Since latency age children have only partially developed a concept of themselves by this stage of psychosocial development, it cannot be expected that they can maintain control for extended periods of time. By the end of the group stage, most older latency age children have focused on working on their individual and group goals and developed some degree of group control. This may be rather fragile and still dependent on the support of the social worker.

If the group is prepared for ending, some of the members may be able to take the controls, which were a part of the expected behavior in the group, and integrate them into their own behavior after the group experience has ended. In this manner, the group is able to support the maturational process that is already occurring with these children.

Norms are expected behaviors. For children, norms are often identified as rules. Very early in the group, the worker may identify some rules and encourage members to add to this list. Even though the list may be very specific, members in the beginning are likely to be very unsure of what is acceptable and wondering who is going to enforce the rules.

In addition, there is another set of norms that is rather covert and tentative at this time. Children may be wondering if all the rules in the classroom also apply in their group. Over time, as the children become more comfortable, they often begin to test the rules to discover if there are real limits on behavior and if the worker or the group is going to enforce them. Usually with younger children, the worker is expected to be the person that follows through to see that rules are followed. To make sure that this happens, the younger children may call the worker's attention to the fact that a rule has been violated and wait for corrective actions to be taken.

Norms may also evolve out of the interactions of the members of the group as described in Chapter 4. The children themselves may be more likely to enforce these newly identified norms because they saw, and perhaps participated in, the process that caused the need to establish a new rule.

Younger latency age children may generally be more accepting of the rules that have been established, and not question them to any great degree. By the third group stage, there may be a few relatively ineffective attempts to really challenge norms, usually by individuals rather than by the group. The changes in norms that do occur are likely to have developed by mutual agreement of the children and the worker, out of the interactions of the members or by the elimination and ignoring of rules. Often, norms identified in the beginning are not necessary or useful as the group develops.

Older latency children, because of psychosocial maturity, may begin to challenge the rules much earlier in group development. Allowing and encouraging the group to question and, where possible, to change the rules is very important in sharing the power of the worker, promoting cohesion and developing a mutual aid system. By the third group stage, the older children can be expected to have developed and modified norms so that there is satisfaction and agreement about them. Finally, as the group and members prepare for separation, the children may selectively decide whether to incorporate or discard the norms of the group.

Goals for children in the beginning are likely to be covert. Probably, having fun is the most overt goal that children bring to groups. This is a very valid goal for children and should be honored; however, it need not be the only end sought. Children often join groups because they are encouraged to do so by parents or friends, or they may be referred by adults in authority positions because of very specific purposes. The social worker and members need to work together to establish goals that are useful and meaningful to the individual child. Certainly, the older latency age children may be more ready to participate actively in this process than younger children.

Initially, the children may need to be exposed to the idea of individual goals related to the general purpose of the group. An example is a group of boys who were referred by the vice-principal at the school for creating problems in the classroom. It can be expected to take some time before the children are willing to admit that they and their behavior played a part in this situation. Often the teacher, other children, the school subject, or someone or something is blamed for the problem. Frequently, it is denied by the children that there is a problem at all. They may agree, however, that they do not "get along" well in school. This can allow the purpose of the group to be "to help them 'get along' better in school." This allows children to begin to identify individual goals that can help them function more appropriately in the school setting.

To understand this process and to develop sufficient trust to expose one's weaknesses, may take until the end of the second stage when some degree of acceptance has been reached among the members. During the stage of "Working on My Goals," the members are more likely to be prepared to focus and work on their own specific aims with the help of the practitioner and the others. By the time of termination, some of the goals will have been attained, but some will not. The practitioner and group need to evaluate the achievements of each member and the group as well as those goals that still may need to be accomplished.

In working with younger children, problem behaviors may often be best identified by observing and assessing members as the group develops. As the children are able, the worker may help them identify specific problems and elicit help from others to assist with the change process.

Roles are made up of clusters of behaviors. On observing the specific clusters of behaviors of a member, it is often possible to identify a role that he/she is taking by giving it a name such as, "leader," "clown," "encourager" or "mediator." These roles may either be functional or dysfunctional for the members and the group. If they help the member and the group move toward their goals, they are viewed as functional and, if not, dysfunctional.

Some roles are essential to the functioning of the group. If a member who plays a specific role such as "focuser" is absent when an important discussion takes place, the group may flounder until another member or the worker steps into that role. Especially with children's groups, it is often the practitioner who plays specific essential roles until a member is able to step into that set of behaviors.

Latency age children in the beginning stage gradually and tentatively take on roles. Over time, as the members get to know each other, there is often an assumption or assignment of roles. Often the most obvious one is that of leader. Sometimes, at least initially, the child does not even know that he/she is playing this role until others make this fact known. In this case, the role has been assigned by the other members to this member. Sometimes, the role may be assumed by a member, such as that of the "clown."

Young latency children, with a few exceptions, may continue in these roles throughout the life of the group. The one role that often can be moved from child to child is the leadership that is related to a specific type of activity. For example, if a group of boys is playing baseball, John may become the leader; however, if the activity shifts to an art project, it may be Tommy who takes over leadership. The practitioner, who is aware of this fact, can often allow opportunities for all the members to take on the leadership role at some point. Sometimes, the least popular member moves into a positive, accepted role when his/her knowledge or ability is discovered by the other members. Perhaps, on a camping trip planned by the group, a boy who is not well accepted by the others is discovered to be an excellent guitar player. The boy's talent in this area allows the children to discover some other positive characteristics about him and, as a result, move him to a much more positive role.

The more mature latency age children may be able to move out of their usual roles and try out others as they begin to focus more clearly on goal accomplishment in the third group stage. As they begin to feel some success in their accomplishments and self-esteem increases, it is easier to give up the old ways of behaving and try out new behaviors and roles. This may continue for these members until the group terminates, and it becomes essential for all the members to relinquish their roles.

Other Structures

In addition to these essential dynamics discussed above, other areas of structure that change over time in groups have also been suggested. Communication patterns in the group are expected to change as the group progresses. In the beginning of latency age groups, it can be expected that there will be a mixed pattern. Some children can be expected to communicate primarily with the worker, others may withdraw and relate only to members or to another child. In the second stage, "Establishing My Place in the Group," the children generally will have become more trusting of each other, the group and the situation so that communication is much freer for most of them. This trend could be expected to continue until termination.

Two other prominent and related areas of change that are expected in any group are problem-solving processes and conflict resolution. Conflict must not be viewed as either "good" or "bad" but rather as "necessary." Generally in the initial stage, little disagreement occurs. Often, if there is disagreement, it is either ignored, passed over or simply agreed to by the others. Some children display "company manners" until they become better acquainted and more trusting of the others.

During the second stage, "Establishing My Place in the Group," conflict may become a major characteristic. It is within this conflict situation that changes in types of resolution may be seen as the group progresses. Eubank (1932) classified societal action into two categories, opposition and accommodation. These two categories can be divided into five types of conflict resolution, including: elimination, subjugation, compromise, alliance and integration. Elimination involves a method in which members combat each other to win and, if necessary, to rid the group of the opposing faction. Subjugation occurs when those with the strongest point of view force others to accept their view. Compromise can be used when the opposing groups have almost equal strength. In this process, those with each point of view may be required to give up something to safeguard the activity or the group. Alliances involve sub-groups or individuals who maintain their independence but combine to achieve a common goal. Integration is often viewed as the highest form or most evolved method of resolving differences. It involves the group arriving at a solution that satisfies each of the members and is better than any of the contending suggestions.

Latency age children may most often experiment with a variety of decision-making processes, depending on the nature of the conflict and the specific members involved as the group progresses. Once in a while, an older, more mature latency age group may be able to develop to the point where the members are capable of making an integrated decision. The style of conflict resolution that is utilized is often related to the progress and stage of the group, beginning with the more primitive methods and gradually moving to more sophisticated patterns that take others into account (Fatout, 1989). A group of older latency children may, in the beginning, use elimination or subjugation as a means of resolving conflicts. The members who are the loudest and the most aggressive get their way. As the group members reach the "Working on Goals" stage, they may have moved to the use of compromise or forming alliances as a means of resolving differences.

When the children have been able to resolve the conflict to everyone's satisfaction, there are often mutual feelings of closeness, satisfaction and warmth. Wilson and Ryland (1949) suggest that it may be conflicts and successful resolution that provide the energy or power to move the group along in its progress. Levine (1979) states that conflict resolution provides the building blocks by which inclusion of the entire group occurs, resulting in cohesion. So, there is a very close relationship between the patterns of conflict resolution and the stage of the group.

MOMENT-TO-MOMENT PROCESS

As indicated in the beginning of this chapter, process can either be described by looking at a group structure and describing the changes that occur over time, or it can be viewed as the moment-to-moment interaction between members of the group. Looking at the structure and the changes over time is especially useful in either evaluating the progress of the group or in predicting where the group may be going next but may not be as useful in attempting to influence the immediate direction that the group is taking.

The focus on moment-to-moment process is especially significant for the social worker because there may be need for intervention to help the group move toward goal attainment. Underlying this use of process is a belief by the social worker that all behavior is meaningful and has a purpose, even if that intent is now known to the persons involved.

This type of practitioner participation can only happen when the worker is involved and very attuned to the actual interactions between members as they occur. It is important that the worker views the current situation, including both verbal and nonverbal communication, with a knowledge and understanding of individual, sub-group and group history. An understanding of the history not only involves knowledge of relationships, interactions, feelings and issues of importance to the members from the beginning of the group but also some attempt to understand a variety of possible reasons for this particular interaction occurring *now*. What is the meaning and intent of the member in bringing up an issue or responding to others in the way he/she does at this time? What are the underlying feelings or motives for this interaction?

As practitioners are able to tune into interactions at this level, they gain more and more knowledge of patterns and intents of the children and of the subtle aspects of specific relationships between members, thereby building more information for individualizing and skillfully intervening in the process in a useful manner.

Sometimes, the group may be ready to move on to the next stage of development, but the worker may not be aware of this until observing processes that transpire in the group at that time. An example of this is evident in a group of ten- and eleven-year-old girls from a very low income neighborhood.

The agency provided a small amount of money at Christmas for the group members. The money could be spent any way the children wished. The girls could decide together what they wanted to do. Some children talked of buying treats for themselves; others wanted to take the money home. There were many suggestions and much discussion about how the money could be spent.

This was a group that was composed of two major subgroups, one that was more aggressive and controlling than the other. The worker was wondering how this issue could ever be resolved. Finally, a member of the less powerful subgroup suggested that they draw names and buy gifts for each other. They all agreed. This was not an unusual idea, but it was very unexpected that the controlling sub-group would agree to the suggestions from the other members.

Names were drawn, again with no conflict. The girls went to a variety store, bought the gifts, brought them back and wrapped them. As the gifts were given out, it became evident to the worker that the conflict that they had been having was resolved by integration. After drawing names, the members had found who had their names and had suggested items that they would like. The girls who wanted treats received them. The two girls from very low income homes had gifts to open at the party but were careful to wrap them again to take home as gifts for their mothers.

This was a fascinating session where relatively little overt conflict was evident, and both major factions of the group came together around the simple suggestion of one member with no further formal discussion. Obviously, there was a great deal of discussion during the purchase of the gifts that allowed for the resolution by integration. The important thing the practitioner was aware of in the process was that this group for the first time had used a different form of conflict resolution than they had ever used before. Integration requires that the members take into consideration the desires and needs of all of the members and that all of the members are satisfied with that decision. The fact that the group was able to function in this manner suggests that the children now had moved into the working stage and could be expected to be more helpful to each other in moving toward their goals. Now the practitioner's planning, interventions and expectations could be modified or changed to more appropriately meet the needs and deal with the issues of a group as it entered this stage of development.

This example illustrates a major change in the functioning of a group. Most process is much less dramatic than this but can be just as significant. When one child verbally attacks another for no obvious reason, the worker needs to look for underlying reasons for this behavior. Did something happen in the session last week? Was there a conflict on the way to the session? Did something happen with one's teacher or mother earlier in the day? It is important for the worker to understand the dynamics that are producing the behavior, in order to help the child deal with the underlying concern and be able to move on.

Understanding process in groups involves comprehension of many dynamics that are happening at the same time. It often requires selective and continual focusing. This is complicated but exceedingly important for the practitioner's understanding, in order to appropriately respond and guide the group in the direction required.

As noted in this chapter, not only the functioning of the group as a whole but also of sub-groups and individuals is important to the success of the whole unit. The attention of the social worker is expected to be focused on all of these levels throughout the life of the group. The next chapter centers attention on work with individual members both in and outside the group, as required.

Chapter 8

Working with Members

Focus on the group does not negate the importance of the individual member. "When the focus is upon interpersonal interaction, neither the individual nor the group is submerged: both are viewed as equally important" (Northen, 1969, p. 53). Each can only be fully understood in terms of the other.

A mutual aid system involves members helping each other. In most instances, there is a connection between a member's specific problem and the general purpose of the group (Shulman & Gitterman, 1986). Not only is the individual concerned about resolving a personal issue, but others in the group are likely to be struggling with similar matters. As members attempt to resolve the problem of an individual, by thinking through, giving suggestions and empathizing, they may also sort out and conclude their own issues of a similar nature. Members may use both individual and group help for different issues as they see fit.

INDIVIDUALIZING

Mutual aid systems constantly move back and forth between emphasis on the member and/or the group as the need arises. A focus on individual problem-solving is a part of the process expected in this system. The social worker needs to individualize the members. This requires an emphasis on the unique and idiosyncratic nature of the person (Vinter, 1974b).

Konopka (1983) describes individualization as one of the specifics of the group work method. It is important that the individual not be lost in the whole but rather be helped to feel as a unique person who can contribute to the whole. Individualization occurs when the needs, abilities and capacities of the members are taken into account as well as the environment surrounding them. The member has many things in common with the others and also has many differences.

Each person in the group needs to be distinguished by the practitioner in terms of distinct psychosocial development, potential for relationships and motivation to participate. This social assessment is an ongoing process as well as a first step in practice.

A part of the assessment of children from the time of the very first interview in preparation for composing a group is awareness of the cultural, racial and ethnic factors. In writing of cultural factors, Allen-Meares (1995) says, "Social workers assessing children must take into account their families' racial and cultural variation, how society responds to them, and how these variations affect functioning and development" (p. 89). According to Katz (1982), children as young as three years of age have already begun to develop attitudes about their own group and others.

The significance of racial ethnic identity to children depends on specific experiential factors, such as homogeneity of their environment, their group's sense of social and economic importance and the extent of prejudice perceived or discrimination experienced. (Garbarino, Stott et al., 1992, p. 98)

In assessing the meaning of ethnicity and culture for children, it is important to remember that there may be more differences in a relatively homogeneous group, such as Native Americans, than there is between two differing ethnic groups. Another significant factor is the degree of Americanization that has occurred. Some characteristics believed to be typical of a particular culture may not exist in a specific family because of the Americanization that has happened. At the same time, certain beliefs and behaviors of children can occasionally be explained by cultural beliefs of the family. Sometimes, a child's resistance to talking about home life or family can be explained by a finding of McAdoo (1977): blacks may be especially reluctant to air the family's "dirty laundry" outside the home.

Children as well as adults may display defensive behaviors, including aggression, withdrawal, rage and passivity in response to cross-racial communication. This may happen both with other members of the group as well as with the worker. The expression of feelings and recognition of differences allow children to explore this area and to gain knowledge and understanding about themselves and others. Social distance between the worker and members can be reduced by the practitioner's ability to feel warmth, genuine concern and empathy for the person regardless of race, color or ethnic background (Kadushin, 1972; Solomon, 1976).

Another group identity that may impact behavior in the social work group is social class. Economic status is usually believed to define social class, but there are behavioral expectations related to social class ranging from educational achievements to table manners (Garbarino, Stott et al., 1992).

It is expected that a child's behavior may well be related to income. There are differences in social classes in the time spent with children, objects for play, the safety of environments and the opportunities to participate in various social groups. Children from more privileged groups may learn to feel and act in an overbearing and superior manner with other groups. This may complicate communication between high- and low-status children.

It is important that the practitioner be aware of the many factors that may influence interaction between the members; at the same time, it is essential that these understandings be applied with caution. "Cultural factors need to be viewed as they interact with psychological and environmental ones in a particular situation" (Northen, 1988, p. 193).

Children, by definition, are dependent on their families. This necessitates an understanding of the family dynamics, where possible, in order to better assess the coping and behavioral skills of the child. Ideally, the assessment should include data from parents, school and even a community agency to understand how well the child is functioning. Another dimension of assessment involves listening, collecting data and observing children both before the group is formed and later, as they function in the group.

Working with the Member in the Group

Vinter (1974c, pp. 18–25) wrote of four specific interventions that can affect change in members. He calls these "direct means of influence." The four types of influences are: the worker as the central person, the worker as a symbol and spokesperson, the worker as the motivator / stimulator and the worker as the executive.

The practitioner as a central person is the object for identification of the members. He/she often encourages, models, empathizes with members' feelings and reinforces behavior. Sometimes, even the worker's appearance can be seen to directly affect the appearance of members. In one instance, the male worker came to a session with a new hair style; the next week, a large portion of the boys in the group had a similar haircut. Similarly, in a group of girls, the practitioner had broken her thumb and was wearing a brace on her hand; by the next session, a member had a version of the brace, saying that her thumb was broken.

These inconsequential acts on the part of the members simply highlight the degree of influence that the social worker may have. This fact emphasizes the importance of the practitioner's "conscious use of him/herself." Not every practitioner comes with the same knowledge, skills and capacities, but it is important to utilize those attributes that match those of the group or those that may stimulate the members to participate in new experiences.

As a symbol and spokesperson, the worker is an agent of legitimate norms and values. The practitioner, as the motivator/stimulator, helps members define their individual goals and assists them in interpreting the psychosocial causes of behavior. As noted by Vinter (1974c, pp. 22–23), "Regardless of age or problems, clients tend to restrict themselves to conventional and familiar activities, to have limited perspectives, and to be less aware of the full potentials offered by their social and physical environment." The worker can show the children new games that can be played with old objects. A grassy hill in Southern California can be made into a toboggan run with the use of discarded cardboard boxes, for example.

As the executive, the worker is often the controller of members' roles. This can occur by the practitioner assigning roles in activities and by differentially responding to a particular member. In assigning roles in activities, the social worker can often help the child move toward individual goal accomplishment. The shy, bashful child may develop new confidence and self-esteem by leading a session of the game "Simon Says" or another activity that allows for control of both him/herself and the other children.

In working with young latency age children, it is essential that the social worker participate in a very active manner to assist the members to make connections between individual and group problem-solving. The role of the practitioner in working with young children can best be described as participating as a conduit that helps make the connections between the members and the group, in attempting to resolve problems. For example, a practitioner who works with a boy that feels sad that his pet has died may turn to others in the group and wonder whether any of them have ever felt like Johnny is feeling. This allows the children to recognize the boy's feelings and assists them in remembering how a sad experience felt for them. Sometimes with these empathetic feelings, children can really make connections that allow them to be helpful to each other.

In early latency, the child's ability in this area may be somewhat limited. As indicated in Chapter 2, young latency age children have not developed sufficiently, especially in terms of identity, to be able to give much attention to the problems and issues of others. Their attention is still very much centered on themselves. It is only as the worker can help the children to make the connections that there is awareness of the similarity of problems and issues between members, and that they may have experienced situations that could be useful in helping others.

A group of young children who had been severely physically abused discovered only over time that they had all been victims of battering. As they became aware of this commonality, the worker could use their collective experiences to solve the issues of concern to individual members. This happened in the situation as follows:

All the children were placed in foster homes waiting to be adopted. One young boy was very agitated about how to answer the many questions from classmates about the difference in names between himself and others in the foster family and about the whole situation of being in a foster home. This allowed the social worker to draw on the experience of other members in making suggestions and working out answers to help this boy come to a solution that was comfortable for him. With the use of discussion, puppets and role-play, some possible alternatives were discovered.

Not only was the child with this problem able to move toward resolution, but others in the group could also explore the issue again and perhaps discover some better answers for themselves and also learn to be more comfortable that they were not alone in their concern about this issue.

Sometimes, older latency children are able to identify a problem of one of their members and help them with it. A group of girls had just moved through the inclusion stage and were ready to work on individual goals:

They had planned that day to roast hot dogs at a local park. As they cooked the hot dogs, there was a great deal of chasing, hitting and rowdy behavior. The girls seemed less interested in the cooking and eating than they had been in the past. Obviously, something else was going on, but what? The worker watched but could not understand the patterns observed.

Then, one member at a time began to unobtrusively approach the worker, asking whether she had been near Gloria that session. Finally, one of them indicated Gloria was having difficulty with body odor. They obviously did not want to confront her directly and seemed very protective of her feelings, but they wanted something done to help her.

The worker assured them that she would talk to Gloria and see if she could be of assistance. That is what the members had wanted to occur. So when the worker announced, as they settled in the van to go home, that Gloria would be last today, no one questioned that this would violate the usual order of rotation used in ending their meetings. They recognized that the worker's purpose was to discuss Gloria's problem with her.

After the others were out of the van, Gloria and the worker discussed the problem and found some alternative solutions. As it turned out, the problem was because the family had been unable to pay the bills, and the water had been turned off. The other members had been understanding and protective because many of them had similar experiences in the past, and at the same time were not yet feeling that they had the power or resources to help Gloria solve her problem.

This was also the first time to really test the social worker's skills and ability to assist a member with a problem. In fact, this situation marked the beginning of the transition into the "Working on Goals" stage.

On occasion, it becomes necessary for the practitioner and the members together to identify the problems of a specific individual. For example, one summer's day, only a few members were available for the group, so Elena brought a friend. These nine- and ten-year-old girls ordinarily did not have guests at their meetings, so at first the interaction between members was slow and cautious.

Elena was short and curt in her responses to the worker from the moment she was picked up in the van. She seemed angry. She was unusually unresponsive to the other members. After arriving at the clubroom, Elena became much more actively hostile, usually responding only to the worker. She did this by cussing the worker in Spanish. She called the worker names that were often distinguishable because of their similarity to English words.

The worker responded by trying to discover why Elena was so angry. She said things such as "I don't know why you are so angry," "I cannot remember anything that happened last week that would make you so mad," and "Please just tell me what is the matter." All of this was to no avail; the angry attack continued for at least thirty to forty-five minutes. The other two regular members present were as shocked as the worker, but they seemed to be enjoying her discomfort.

Finally, the guest responded to Elena that she had better "shut up" or the worker was going to "kick her out." The practitioner immediately responded, "Not at all. Obviously, Elena is having some sort of problem and the purpose of the group is to help members with such issues."

Elena immediately relaxed slightly and began to tell how her mother had assured her that she would never take the younger children and leave Elena with her father and older sister. That is what had happened, and Elena had thus begun to question her ability to trust any adult. She had spent the session trying to test whether she could really trust the practitioner. On discovering that she could, she was able to further express her devastation about her mother leaving her behind.

A combination of feelings on the part of Elena seemed to require that she reassure herself that the social worker could be trusted even when her mother could not. An additional impetus for these feelings and behaviors was also the regression in the group that is expected to occur when a nonmember is present.

In this instance, it required most of the session for the worker and group to discover the problem that Elena was having. It was thus necessary to spend extra time with her that day and to schedule other conferences to further identify and clarify the situation and to look for a variety of possible solutions.

As noted by Garvin (1981, pp. 149–150), after a one-to-one encounter in the group, it is important for the practitioner to be aware of factors previous to the encounter, such as the following: Could another member act with the same intent as the worker? Should the total group be asked to participate in the discussion? What does the member in question want in terms of a response? Will the member's actions facilitate or hinder the progression of the group?

During an interaction with an individual member, the worker needs to be aware of the other members' response to the situation. Are they supportive of the worker or are they reacting negatively? Do members join with the worker and initiate discussion of events similar to the one being discussed? After the encounter, what are the long-term effects on the group?

In working on problem-solving with Elena in the group, the worker was aware that she had to respond to her and that the members were also involved and "shocked" by the attack on the worker. The long-term outcome in this situation was the movement of the group into the stage focused on individual and group goals.

Focus on the Child Outside the Group

There are some differences of opinion among group workers regarding the use of one-to-one contacts with members and others in the environment. The position that is taken here is that since the focus is working with children, it is essential that each member and his/her parents be included in the process. The primary concern of those practitioners who oppose this stance is a fear that the individual contact will dilute the power of the group process. Some believe that this contact will undermine the contract that members should help one another. Certainly that is a concern as stated by Northen (1988, p. 255), "A great deal of analytical judgment is necessary to decide wisely whether to deal with the concern privately with the member or to encourage the person to bring the concern into the group."

Interviews are used often when the group is being composed to assess potential members and to prepare and orient them for participation. This individual contact with the worker is also expected to begin a relationship with the child so that entry into the group will become easier. This relationship between the worker and the child can act as a bridge and a connection to the group until the child has made socioemotional ties with the other members.

Another use of the interview is to help members cope with pressing problems that seem unsuitable for discussion in the group. This may be due to the timing as related either to the group or to the member. Often, the worker becomes aware of the need for an interview as a member requests it or is unclear about a problem, or as the worker casually talks to the member or significant others in what Wilson and Ryland (1949, p. 76) call a "curbstone conference."

Other uses of interviews include referring a member to another service, continuing individualization of a child and keeping in contact with a parent(s) of a young child. Sometimes in working with children, the worker schedules regular conferences with each child and at least one home visit with every family during the life of the group. This individual interview allows the practitioner to concentrate attention on one person or system rather than focusing on a multitude of differing systems at one time.

Wilson and Ryland (1949, pp. 24–25) assure us that

in all these situations in which the social group worker comes into a face-to-face relationship with individuals, he is not doing social case work; rather, he is using his skills as a professional social worker in serving both the group-as-a-whole and its component individuals through the use of the face-to-face relationships essential to the practice of social group work.

In working with young latency children, the worker finds that there is insufficient socio-emotional development for the members to share some problems with the group and to expect others to help them problem-solve. It is usually more important that the practitioner is aware of the child's situation and then is able to include other members (with the permission of the child) to help discuss and problem-solve those issues that they are capable of handling.

With older latency children, there may be a range of abilities, skills and readiness to assist each other in solving problems due to the unevenness of psychosocial development between the members. This is an area that the worker must explore and assess in order to know when and how to involve the group in helping resolve problems of a member. It is very possible that by late latency most of the children are capable of assisting. This may result in the worker gaining information in an individual conference and encouraging the member to bring the issue to the group at the next session.

In working with children, the worker often becomes aware of problems in the group not by discussions but rather by observing interactions and behaviors. These brief interviews between the worker and the member are referred to by Redl (1959) as "life space interviews." They may take place immediately before, after or during a session.

Young children often wish to have an opportunity to relate to, and gain the attention of, the social worker on an individual basis. In addition, they are often pleased to have the practitioner and parents jointly focus their attention on them.

In the beginning of the group, if a part of the purpose is to help members "get along better," then the overall purpose of the conference can be explained and interpreted in this context, along with a more specific purpose. The member then understands that the social worker is there to help rather than to get him/her into trouble. Before a conference is scheduled, it is usually wise to make the child aware of the plan and the expected content and to invite him/her to participate. This makes the member feel supported by the worker and further establishes a sense of trust.

In working with children of any age, it is important to emphasize again and again in a wide variety of ways that the purpose is always to help them, not to get them into trouble in any way, although this may happen if a child is doing something to hurt him/herself or others. In this context, it is important for the worker to let the children know he/she will want to have conferences with them throughout the life of the group. This is one way that the practitioner can get to know and be of more assistance to the members. Each child will have a turn to see the worker, but there may be occasions when one member needs more help than usual and that someone may be seen more often than another. This will not happen because the worker likes that child more, but rather because that member needs more help at that time. This type of explanation has been found to be helpful in eliminating most jealousy and sibling rivalry that could otherwise be expected. This understanding was clear enough to one group, that on its termination, members sent a card saying how much they missed their club and how much it meant to them, but they knew that other children now needed the help of the worker.

During one of the get-acquainted conferences, one member disclosed some important information about her problem in an area in which she really needed help but had been unable to ask for it directly:

Lucy said that when she goes to a local movie theater, she always gets into trouble with other children and the theater employees. She knew her behavior was "wild" and out of control. She told of one night when her father came to the theater, caught her and made her stop her negative behavior. She smiled as she told this, expressing a great deal of love and respect for him. She seemed to be extremely pleased that he cared enough about her to stop her destructive behavior.

With this in mind, the practitioner remembered how many times she felt guilty because Lucy was "wilder" on the way home from the session than she had been at the beginning of that meeting. She would begin to "act out" and be encouraged by the others to continue. When this occurred, there was a buildup and Lucy was unable to stop her actions despite worker's efforts. Although Lucy was serving a purpose for the others in the group—to express some of their negative feelings—it was destructive for her.

When realizing that Lucy wanted and needed support to behave differently, the worker asked, "Are you saying that you want me to help you stop this behavior in the group?" Lucy nodded her head, "yes". After some discussion and a decision about what the worker could do to be of assistance in this matter, steps were taken in the next sessions to help change her behavior. In the beginning, it was felt that the other members were unable to actively support this new behavior because it served their needs; however, as Lucy changed over time, they understood her desire to be different and they, too, began to help.

The other group members were unable to help Lucy in the beginning because of the contagion that was occurring; Lucy stimulated the others, and they excited her. It was not until Lucy, with the help of the worker, could better her own behavior, that the other members could also help with her problem.

Until the time of the individual conference, the practitioner had observed Lucy's behavior as a problem that affected herself and the group but was not aware that Lucy also perceived it as an issue of concern. If an individual conference had not been scheduled, it might have been some time before the worker realized that Lucy was ready to make changes. The relationship between the worker and Lucy was clarified and enhanced during this individual session. Previous to the conference when the worker attempted to stop Lucy's behavior, it seemed only to spiral her behavior to a higher level. She seemed to perceive the practitioner's attempted interventions as acts of authority rather than as efforts to help. After the conference, with a clearer understanding of the worker's role and honest interest in her, Lucy seemed to view the practitioner as a team member who could help her control her behavior.

Sometimes, caution must be taken to further clarify the worker's role and use of individual interviews so that they are not misused by the member. At a later time, Lucy asked the worker to talk with her parents to gain approval for her to attend a party of which they had not approved. The worker indicated that she did not know enough about Lucy's behavior at parties and did not feel free to intervene with her parents. This opened a discussion in the group of how Lucy and others behaved at social functions and did not lead to further intervention in this matter with Lucy's parents.

Another way in which children may instigate individual interviews is by using a very informal method. One child (Jill) in a residential treatment center simply presented herself at the worker's office just before the group session. Jill was a young child who had been rejected by her mother and siblings and was not well accepted by peers in this institutional setting. At first she only stopped at the worker's office to walk with her to the group session, but as time passed, she came earlier and earlier.

As Jill found that she was accepted and cared about, "the visits" were used to help establish a positive relationship between her and the worker. At a later time, the worker could use this positive relationship, which had been developed, to help support Jill's acceptance by the others. For example, as Jill entered the group and members fussed at her (or she felt that they did), the worker pulled a chair up next to her and indicated very quietly that she would like to sit next to Jill today. This must be done with caution and not too often, so that feelings of sibling rivalry are not aroused in other members. If the interpretation is given that Jill is having difficulties today and the group needs to see if it can help her, it further involves the others in a positive, altruistic manner.

It is important for the worker to use the interview to meet the needs of the individual and, at the same time, not detract from the group as the primary means of service. In the examples described above, the practitioner used the relationship that was developed with Jill to assist her in bringing the problems of concern back into the group for discussion and problem-solving.

As suggested by Shulman (1986), individual sessions can be used to aid a child to raise an issue in the group. Sometimes, at first the material seems too personal to talk about in the group context. As it is discussed in individual conferences and not harshly judged, the child is encouraged to discuss his/her concern in the group (Indelicato & Goldberg, 1986).

It can be concluded that conferences with individuals are an important and integral part of social work practice with groups, along with the interactions and processes that occur. "The ultimate test of effectiveness of social work practice is the extent to which the persons who were served have made positive changes toward the goals set with them, associated with the group experience" (Northen, 1988, p. 224).

Conferences with Families and Collaterals

The amount of individual contact with families of the group members is dependent on the age and developmental level of the child as well as the nature of the problem of concern. After explaining to the child the constructive purpose of contacts with families, the practitioner often allows the child to assist in determining the need and desirability of having such a contact.

Often in working with children, material for assessment purposes has been gathered from the schools. After identifying to the school the worker's and agency's interest in a particular child and perhaps also focusing attention on him/her, it is important to continue this contact with the school in the future. Not only does this promote good public relations with the educational systems, but it may be of great help both to the practitioner and to the principals and teachers in working with the child in the future.

Both the school and the child need to know that only broad descriptions of group activity and individual behaviors will be shared with those in the school system, and that this is the type of feedback from the school that is desired by the worker. The intent is to promote the trust of both the members and those in the school systems.

SUMMARY

The child needs to know that contacts will be made with the school from time to time, again, with the broad purpose of helping the child rather than causing harm.

Individual work with the child, both within and outside the group as well as through collateral contacts with significant others, is an important aspect of social work as described in this chapter. It is clear, as the variety of means of helping members change are identified, that working with groups is a very complex and challenging method for helping clients. In addition, there are modifications that must be made in some of the usual processes in order to provide service to children.

These complexities that have occurred in previous stages continue into the next group phase, the ending stage. As described in the final chapter, there are some unusual and interesting interactions that can be expected to happen as a children's group prepares for ending.

Chapter 9
Ending the Group

A description of the group and members has moved through the first three stages and is now entering the final one, the ending. The feelings and behaviors related to termination may occur when a worker leaves the group, an individual terminates, the total group ends and even when there is an interruption of the group sessions for a period of time. In working with children in a school setting, a holiday or school vacation that causes the discontinuance of the group for a week or two may produce the hostility and anger associated with endings. As a result, the practitioner must be aware that children need to be carefully prepared for vacation periods when the group will not be meeting. Sometimes, even when this has been accomplished, some of these feelings are expressed and must be worked through as the group comes back together.

There are a number of possible reasons for ending a group that are identified as follows: goals have been reached, a predetermined time has arrived, the group is unsuccessful and has not gelled and the group's mechanisms for coping are maladaptive and it cannot function as a therapeutic system (Johnson, 1974; Northen, 1988; Sarri & Galinsky, 1974).

The members' responses to the ending of the group may vary depending on an assortment of circumstances, such as the length of service, the structure of the group, past experiences with loss and separation, reasons for termination, the depth of meaningful relationships and the degree of support in the environment (Northen, 1988). One might wonder about the dynamics of endings in short-term groups. What are they like? After reviewing the literature, Levine (1979, p. 242) concluded that "The dynamics of the termination phase for short-term and long-term groups is similar but the depth of those dynamics differ with the length and depth of the process." The possible importance of endings for some is emphasized by Yalom (1985) in his statement, "termination is thus more than an extraneous event in the group; it is the microcosmic representation of some of the most crucial and painful issues of all" (p. 373).

THE MEANING OF ENDINGS FOR CHILDREN

The effect of termination on children's groups certainly will depend on the experience of the individual child up to that point. For most young latency age children, the group may simply be a step in their new adventure of exploring the world outside the family unit. As noted by Mahler (1968), for others who have not completed the stage of separation-individuation, termination may create real difficulties and may feel like they are being torn apart. Generally as children are beginning school, they are developmentally just beginning to relate in more meaningful ways to other children. Up to this time, almost all their focus has been on themselves. During the group, the practitioner often attempts to help them begin to develop an interest and concern regarding other members. As noted by Levine (1979), even older latency age children can only achieve a limited amount of mutuality. With latency children, therefore, the degree of mutuality that exists will be dependent on the therapist. The latency age children "will remain very dependent on the therapist for keeping open freedom for diversity and deviance from the group in thoughts, feelings, and behavior" (Levine, 1979, p. 77). Developmentally, the child in the working stage of the group is only able to achieve surface or shallow mutuality and generally not as devastated by the ending of the group.

At the same time, the relationship with the worker may be the most important concern for other children. Many will view the worker as another adult, like a teacher, police officer and other people with roles and functions different from their parents, which only adds to their expanding view of the world. For other children who have been abused and neglected, the social worker and group may provide the "testing ground" and "lab" for "trying out" the responses of new adults and their behaviors in relation to themselves.

In working with a group of severely abused children, a most interesting aspect of the group interactions was the childrens' exploration and testing of the co-leaders. One group consisted of five boys and girls and two social work interns. The children's investigation and testing of the practitioners and their responses included focusing on the workers' physical characteristics, such as touching their hair, rubbing their nylon hose, sitting on their laps and carefully examining jewelry. The members also tested the workers' response to their behavior, which included fighting with each other and competing for close proximity to an adult as well as carefully calculated behaviors such as pouring punch down the skirt of the worker. They also explored other areas of the co-leaders' lives, such as whether they were married or had children. Since the children had been abused, they were also very interested in which of the two co-leaders had power. One child approached this by simply asking the two adults, ''Who is the boss?''

One might wonder why a group was important to a child who, because of having been victimized, was also suffering from developmental delays. There were clearly gains that were made in the members' relationships with each other while in the group that could be expected to assist them in their movement toward more ''normal'' developmental expectations. Even more important was the opportunity to explore and test authority figures in a safe environment. They were in a setting with other children present, so it did not seem as frightening (because of safety in numbers). It also provided an environment in which a child could take a risk while others observed the worker's response, thus allowing one member to test the worker's response for others.

These children, because of their moves from foster home to foster home, had developed defenses that prevented them from becoming too emotionally attached either to each other or the workers. This resulted in their relating to others more as objects rather than as people and caused little response to the termination of the group. They seemed to accept ending as the expected outcome. They had been prepared early in the group for this event and seemed to accept it with quiet resignation. It can only be hoped that the children gained enough from this experience, that they could approach a new group situation more confidently because of the knowledge and skills developed.

Learning to cope with loss is an essential part of life. Termination of groups can often assist members to deal with previous losses in their lives; however, these children, because of the severity of losses at a very early stage in their lives and the many resulting complications and problems, were only able at this time to use the defense mechanisms that they had used before to protect themselves.

Older latency age children may be much more affected by termination, especially if the group has been longer-term (perhaps lasting for a year or more). Often in these groups, the children have developed very significant and meaningful relationships with each other and with the practitioner, so the ending means simultaneously losing the worker and sometimes a significant number of friends.

Themes, Feelings and Behaviors Related to Endings

The dissolution of any relationship is marked by a series of emotions, some of which are positive and affirming, others, negative and denying of the experience and many of them contradictory (Henry, 1992). The range of themes during termination are identified as: denial, flight, regression, expressing a need to continue, recapitulation, review and evaluation (Garland, Jones & Kolodny, 1965).

Denial is a defense mechanism to block out painful situations or events and is a very common manner of dealing with ending the group. Usually in forming the group, the practitioner identifies a time for ending services. In working with children's groups, termination is often linked with another period of time in the members' lives, such as the end of the semester or the school year or during the summer break. Often, this seems to make termination easier for the children. They are more aware of endings in a broader context (e.g., the end of the school year) and therefore more cognizant that the group will be ending at the same time.

Some group workers have argued that emphasis on endings at the beginning of the group may prevent members from engaging themselves in the process wholeheartedly. Children appear not to be as affected by this as more mature persons might be. The children's retention of this information fades quickly as their enthusiasm for the group and its activities expands. At the same time, there is an awareness that when the semester or year is over, the group ends. The child's perception of time also influences the lack of concern about termination in the future: for a child, it seems so far away.

To allow opportunities for group members to work through the feelings of denial, it is important for the worker to plan when to remind the children that the group will be ending. Some of the factors to consider in making this decision are: how long the group has been together, the purpose of the group, the amount of cohesion that has developed and the accomplishment of goals.

The response to the mention of the ending of the group may be silence and no reaction as if the subject had not been mentioned (described in Chapter 1). Other responses may be, "Oh, no! We just got started," or "Why do we have to end so soon?" After termination is mentioned, it is helpful to allude to it in a casual way from week to week.

Often, in order to focus more clearly on the fact that the group *will* be ending, it is important to involve the members in planning for the last session. This focus on the reality of ending creates a time and a space for dealing with a variety of feelings. With young latency children, it is sometimes useful to use a calendar or some other item to show how many more weeks are left and when the last meeting will be held. A visual representation may be more meaningful for them.

Denial often continues at some level until the very last session. In the process of working through this stage, children often decide that their group really does not have to end, that a mother or some other adult will appear to lead them after the worker is gone. The children may cluster together against the "bad" worker who is leaving them even though they still need him/her. This idea is often proposed, but details are not worked out, allowing it to remain a vague hope to the end. If the worker attempts to assist the children in looking at the reality of this plan, the response is additional defensiveness and clustering from the worker.

Flight is another common response to the first mention of the group ending. In a few instances, a member may not return to the group at the next session. It may be important to make contact with that child and encourage a return to the next week's meeting. The purpose of this is to allow the child to work through the separation in a positive manner. Sometimes, a child may be unwilling to return, making excuses of not having time to come or of having more interesting activities outside the group. Others may continue to attend but on a less regular basis than before. This latter method for dealing with endings is probably a much healthier one. These members are making connections with other children outside the group but usually attend sessions often enough to reduce some of the attachment to others. Most of the members will be discussing outside activities more and telling of new friendships.

Another manifestation of flight is often the devaluing of the group and the whole experience. Children may say such things to each other as, "The group was no good anyhow. It was dumb!" and "You guys just goofed around. We never did anything." Or, they may say to the worker, "You get paid for this? My mother will do it for nothing." This is their way of attempting to separate from the people and experiences with the least immediate hurt for themselves.

Regression is another very common theme as groups end. Often, behaviors that were problems in an early stage now reappear as the group is about to terminate. The message communicated by this behavior seems to be, "See, we still need you." Usually, this message is targeted both to the other group members and the practitioner. A poignant example of this occurred in a group of older latency girls that was about to end. Several of the members had been referred to the group because of shoplifting:

The girls had planned to go to the local beach for their last group session. When it was time to meet, the weather was cloudy, misty and unpleasant. They insisted that it might be different at the beach and that they had to go. The worker reluctantly agreed. Weather conditions were no different at the beach, and everyone started to return to the clubroom.

The girls had brought money and asked to stop at a little market to spend it. At first, only a few members left the van to go, then a few more. They were gone for a longer time than seemed necessary, so the worker entered the market to see if everything was alright. The girls seemed to enjoy the fact that the worker had come to look for them. They were smiling and acting very evasive, almost as if they were poised to run. Some were standing at the counter waiting to pay for their items. The worker, now feeling more assured, returned to the van to await their return.

When they returned, they pretended to talk among themselves but made sure the worker could hear. The suggestion was that they had been shoplifting. When gently confronted by the worker, this was not the case at all. The purpose of the pretense, as explained by them, was to play a joke on the worker.

Since some of the girls had entered the group because of shoplifting, this was a way to demonstrate their ongoing need for the group and to give the worker the impression, that this was still a problem.

Another theme that is very related to regression is the "need to continue." This need is often demonstrated in a variety of ways. With children, it is probably most often acted out, as in the example above. Another very common way to communicate this message is by exposing another major problem that a member or group is experiencing. Sometimes, this is done by communicating to the group about a new problem or sometimes it is acted out. Often, this behavior is referred to as "doorknob therapy." It is the type of behavior that occurs with adults when the client has one hand on the doorknob ready to leave for the last time and says something such as, "I decided last night I was going to get a divorce."

An example of this theme occurred with a group of older latency boys who had planned to spend their last session on an outing in a wooded area. They had been warned about the danger of fire because of the dry conditions. While on their outing, they did start a fire. It was quickly quenched, but the boys certainly had the attention of the worker and the authorities. This seemed to be another example of "We still need the group!"

These examples have presented behaviors that are extreme but are intended to clearly illustrate the purposes for which they are being utilized. For many children, indications of their continuing need for the group are much more subtle and almost unnoticeable, unless one is very focused on looking for possible meanings of this type of behavior.

Recapitulation is another theme in the ending of the group, especially if it has met over a long period of time. Sometimes, this is worked out through reenactment of earlier experiences. In other situations, there can be a verbal reviewing of experiences. Members begin to clearly see the changes in behavior and their thoughts about each other. Sometimes near the end of the group, members begin to spontaneously reminisce about what each other and the group were like in the beginning. If this process is not just initiated by members, it often is stimulated as the practitioner and members begin evaluating whether goals have been attained. Younger latency age children are much more limited in this ability because of their developmental stage.

One group of older latency age girls had meet for a two-year period and wanted to express their feelings to the social worker at the end of the group:

Two representatives of the group arrived at the worker's home and handed her an envelope. They seemed embarrassed and quickly left saying, "Look in your back yard." The worker opened the envelope to find a Mother's Day card signed by all the members on which they had written a message about how much she had been like a mother to them. In the back yard was a statue of a lion as a gift.

The girls had been unable to directly tell the worker how they felt about her but rather chose to do it with a card. (It would have been interesting to hear the process that went into the selection of this type of card.) It might be expected that a great deal of recapitulation was involved as the group members attempted to decide what variety of card to purchase.

An informal review and evaluation of the group (worker and members) is often begun in the process of recapitulation. If it is not initiated by the group, the social worker introduces the process. It is important for members to understand gains that they have made that can be taken with them as they leave the group and that can be applied to other relationships. (This is discussed further later in the chapter.)

Feelings and Behaviors

As the practitioner recognizes the many themes that are being played out, underlying feelings often become evident. The feelings that accompany endings are described as being like those that occur with death and mourning. Sometimes, there is grief and sadness often covered over by defensive and denying behaviors. Other feelings often experienced are denial (we aren't really ending), anger, rejection, bargaining behaviors, depression, guilt and other painful, negative feelings. At the same time, for many there are also some positive feelings, perhaps ones that are overlooked initially because of the emphasis on the negative aspects.

Positive, or at least ambivalent, feelings associated with endings are those of success, pleasure at attainment of goals and sometimes relief that more time will be "freed up" to do other things.

Most children are only able to express these feelings through behavior. The behaviors sometimes are overt, and the underlying feelings are very subtle. One group of older girls seemed to work out a variety of feelings in the very last session:

They were in the van on the way back to the clubroom when they passed a neighborhood park. Up to that point, the members had been unusually quiet and withdrawn from each other and the worker. They asked if they could stop and go to the park until it was time for the group to end. The worker told them when they would need to return to the van to be taken home. That time arrived, and four of the members were not there. Others reported that they had seen these four leaving the park earlier. This had never happened before and was of great concern to the worker. After what seemed an eternity, they did return to the van. They were nonchalant and defensive and seemed to be waiting for the scolding of the worker. As the worker associated this behavior to feelings about ending, she talked about how she could understand their anger at her and the whole group. This statement allowed the others, too, to again express their feelings.

Some of the feelings in this group had been worked through earlier, but as the last meeting approached, there had been a buildup of feelings for all of the girls. Obviously, they were expressing anger at the worker, but there were many other feelings also. They were trying their new freedom to violate the rules of the club by leaving the park as they wished and by not complying with the request of the worker to return to the van at a particular time. Their nonchalant concern about their behavior indicated an independence from the worker and the group, in terms of approval or disapproval of their behavior.

The other members also seemed surprised and almost shocked by the behavior of these four girls. At the same time, they seemed to be closely observing and enjoying the interaction between these girls and the worker. It was a way to test their independence from the worker and the others by experiencing through the behaviors of others.

In this same group, the behavior of one of the girls again conveys some of her underlying feelings:

The girls were taken home in a rotating fashion, changing from session to session. Each of them always wanted to be last. Lydia was one of the girls who had acted out in the earlier description. It was not her turn to be last, but she manipulated the others so that she was last, by pretending to return to a girl's house to get her coat. (The coat was later found in the back of the van.)

During the group, Lydia had been in the far back seat of the van; as the others left, she moved to the front passenger's seat. As the practitioner and Lydia approached her house, she very quickly slipped over in the seat and kissed the worker on the cheek and just as quickly opened the car door and ran for her house.

This seemed to be Lydia's way of expressing caring, a "thank you" to the worker and, perhaps, even a little guilt over her earlier behavior.

Positive feelings related to group endings often culminate in plans for a special party, an activity, a trip or some special celebration. This period is intended to remember only the most positive aspects of the group and is referred to by Schwartz (1974) as the "farewell party syndrome." Usually, this celebration of successes is an exciting period of affirmation, but for some groups, which have tended to "act out," it is important for the worker to be aware that sometimes all of the negative feelings of the members may not have been worked out. This may result in a crisis even at the final session. Planning for these instances may emphasize meeting in a familiar, relatively safe environment so unexpected behaviors can be better controlled and handled.

WORKER'S ROLE IN ENDINGS

The practitioner is preparing him/herself, the members and the group as a whole for the termination. As the members are reminded of the specific time when the group will be ending, there may be specific changes in their behavior. Sometimes, in the beginning, there is an increased urgency to work on problems because of the lack of time. If this occurs with children, it is usually rather short-lived. It may be used as a reason why the group should not end.

The termination is going to represent a loss for individual members and, as noted by Berman-Rossi (1993, p. 78), "In the face of loss, an approach/avoidance pattern returns." This pattern of behavior is very similar to the beginning stage.

The mutuality that has developed subsides, and members tend to withdraw from facilitating each other. They no longer are interested in encouraging others to express feelings or in giving and receiving feedback. The children are more likely than ever to be preoccupied with their own concerns about separation. So, the role behaviors that previously have been evident now disappear. As described by Henry (1992, p. 198), "Members are returning from group orientation to self orientation." As a result, differentiated role behaviors may cease to be performed.

The worker returns to the role that he/she occupied in the beginning stage, that of moving back to a central position. This move is intended to help the children disconnect from each other. The energy of the children is redirected away from the collectivity and toward themselves as individuals.

It is important to remember that the social worker may experience some of the same feelings as the children at the time of termination. These feelings of sadness, regret, guilt, relief and success may render the practitioner very vulnerable as the children work through their ambivalences. As a result, very early in the termination process, it is important that the social worker carefully evaluate his/her work with the group, the goal accomplishments of the children and the group as a whole. After this is completed, the practitioner can be very clear about which of the criticisms made by the children are genuine and which are expressions due to feelings about endings. After the worker has honestly evaluated his/her performance, then total attention can be focused on the feelings expressed by the children without becoming defensive.

If workers do not carefully evaluate their own work and make some decisions about what they did well or wished they had done differently, their feelings and emotions could get caught up in the attacks that may be made by the children and further confuse this ending process.

Another issue that may be of concern to workers is self awareness (Levine, 1979). If workers have unresolved feelings regarding separations or endings from earlier in their life, then certainly it will be more difficult to deal with their own feelings as well as those of the group.

Processes Essential to Termination

Termination is viewed as a very important process. It is just as important as any other group stage and perhaps even more crucial. This is the opportunity for the practitioner to help the members stabilize gains that they have made, so they can continue to function in the world outside the group by using the skills and understanding that they have gained.

Usually, a first step in this process is to involve the children in evaluating their experience, including their participation, the accomplishment of their goals, the group content and the worker's performance. As described earlier, the reminiscing that sometimes happens spontaneously as endings are discussed may be used as a starting point for more serious evaluation.

If the children do not naturally move into a form of evaluation, then the worker needs to be prepared to help them accomplish this. If the children are capable of sitting quietly and discussing, this method could be used. Usually more creative means are necessary to really involve all of the group members.

A possible way of getting young children involved in the evaluation might be to have them pretend that they have boarded a train and are preparing to leave. Chairs may be lined up to imitate seats on a train. All the children individually say "good-bye" to their completed experience and tell what they liked about their visit and what they would have liked to have been different. They might also be asked to tell what they would want to happen if they went on another trip of this type in the future. Many creative and inviting games and activities can be invented that involve the children in the fun as they also evaluate their experiences.

In this process, there needs to be some focus on achievement of treatment goals, a review of accomplishments and disappointments, an evaluation of the practitioner and an opportunity to recognize, and perhaps deal with, unfinished business. As these areas of concern are being addressed, many of the feelings about endings are being played out, experienced and discussed.

As the group ends, concerns of the worker are helping the children maintain beneficial changes, continue to use their skills, attitudes and knowledge gained and, when appropriate, seek out and use new services.

Play and activities as a way to assist in endings. Along with discussion and preparation for endings, it is also important for the worker to plan activities that do not promote the further development of cohesion. From the very first group stage, the practitioner has been working to develop and promote cohesion. Now in the termination stage, it is important to reverse the course and to think about and utilize means to break down the cohesive bonds that have evolved.

The factors that need to be considered when the group is terminating are: the activity to be used must be one in which success is assured, it needs to be one which clearly reduces cohesion, and it needs to help the group reach beyond the group for satisfaction (Johnson, 1974).

It may be difficult to ascertain which activity will be successful with the group. Sometimes, it is wisest to repeat an activity that had been especially successful and enjoyable earlier in the group. Another possibility is to plan a number of possible activities so that an alternative one can be readily available as necessary. One may want to rely on members to suggest things that they want to do.

The second consideration in regard to program in the ending stage emphasizes the use of activities that do not promote cohesion and perhaps tend to reduce cohesion. A major factor to analyze is whether the program planned requires teamwork or sharing behaviors. For example, it would be inappropriate for the group to make a mural together, because sharing of ideas, crayons and space promotes cohesion. An alternative might be to give each child a piece of paper and a box of crayons and ask every member to draw where he/she might be and what he/she might be doing at this same time next week when the group is no longer meeting. This directs the attention to the fact that the group is ending and helps the members think of things they could be doing outside their regular session, by focusing on their functioning in the community.

A final consideration in thinking about program at the time of termination is helping members reach beyond the group for satisfaction. Activities need to be focused on doing things that are possible to do without the other group members. Again, team activities may not be available in their own neighborhood without the rest of the group. Perhaps a substitute might be to play miniature golf, where only one companion may be needed. Even a hike in the woods is an activity that may be enjoyable for a child without companionship. These activities can be done as a group during termination and, in this way, expose the children to new experiences that they may continue to do without the others.

As indicated earlier, often during one of the very last sessions, the children want to have a party. This activity often provides a helpful setting for reinforcing some of the members' attitudes toward endings. Some part of the party can be used to remind them of goals achieved and accomplishments that each has made. This may be done verbally or may involve certificates of achievement similar to a graduation ceremony. Choosing the way to accomplish this needs to be thought through by the practitioner, keeping in mind the potential meaning for that particular group and its members. Feedback may even be focused on how they could use new skills and attitudes in their future, again attempting to reduce their dependence on each other and emphasizing their performance as individuals.

The small group is utilized to assist children in accomplishing developmental goals as well as for prevention and rehabilitation. Help is given using a mutual aid system and group processes as well as through the behaviors of the worker(s). As goals are accomplished and gains are stabilized, the child returns to life outside the group. Careful planning and work with the children in this final stage is essential to complete the group process and prepare the members to function without the support of the group. As a result, it is essential for the practitioner to give full attention and thoughtfulness to this ending process.

References

Alissi, A. S. (1980). Social group work: Commitment and perspective. In A. S. Alissi (Ed.), *Perspectives on social group work practice* (pp. 5–33). New York: The Free Press.

Alissi, A. S. (1981). The social group work method: Toward a reaffirmation of essentials. In N. N. Goroff (Ed.), *Reaping from the field from practice to principle: Proceedings of social work group three—1981* (Vol. 2). N.p.

Allen-Meares, P. (1995). *Social work with children and adolescents.* White Plains, NY: Longman.

Bateson, G. (1976). A theory of play and fantasy. In J. S. Bruning, A. Jolly, and K. Syla (Eds.), *Play: Its role in development and evolution* (pp. 119–129). New York: Basic Books.

Berger, L. (1974). *From instinct to identity.* Englewood Cliffs, NJ: Prentice-Hall.

Berman-Rossi, T. (1993). The tasks and skills of the social worker across stages of group development. *Social Work with Groups, 16* (1/2), 69–81.

Bertcher, H. J. & Maple, F. (1978). *Creating groups.* Beverly Hills, CA: Sage.

Bruner, J., Jolly, A. & Sylva, K. (1976). *Play: Its role in development and evolution.* New York: Basic Books.

Cartledge, G. & Milburn, J. F. (1981). *Teaching social skills to children.* Elmsford, NY: Pergamon Press.

Churchill, S. (1959). Pre-structuring group content. *Social Work, 4* (3), 52–59.

Cohen, D. H. (1972). *The learning child.* New York: Pantheon.

Coll, B. D. (1970). *Perspectives in public welfare: A history.* Washington, DC: U.S. Department of Health, Education and Welfare, Demonstration and Training, Intramural Research Division.

Erikson, E. H. (1963). *Childhood and society* (2d. ed.). New York: W. W. Norton.

Eubank, E. (1932) *The concept of sociology.* New York: D. C. Health & Company.

Fatout, M. F. (1975). A comparative analysis of practice concepts described in social work literature. Dissertation, University of Southern California.

Fatout, M. F. (1989). Decision-making in therapeutic groups. *Groupwork, 2* (1), 70–79.

Fatout, M. F. (1992). *Models for change in social group work.* New York: Aldine de Gruyter.

Fatout, M. F. (1993). Physically abused children: Activity as a therapeutic medium. *Social Work with Groups, 16* (3), 83–96.

Flavell, J. H. (1985). *Cognitive development* (2d. ed.). Englewood Cliffs, NJ: Prentice-Hall.

Freud, A. (1965). *Normality and pathology in childhood.* New York: International Universities Press.

Garbarino, J., Stott, F. M. & Faculty of Erikson Institute (1992). *What children can tell us.* San Francisco: Jossey-Bass.

Garland, J. A. & West, J. (1984). Differential assessment and treatment of the school age child: Three group approaches. *Social Work with Groups, 7* (4), 57–70.

Garland, J. A., Jones, H. E. & Kolodny, R. L. (1965). A model for stages of development in social work groups. In S. Bernstein (Ed.), *Explorations in group work* (pp. 17–71). Boston: Boston University School of Social Work.

Garvey, C. (1977). *Play.* Cambridge, MA: Harvard University Press.

Garvin, C. D. (1981). *Contemporary group work.* Englewood Cliffs, NJ: Prentice-Hall.

Garvin, C. D. (1987). *Contemporary group work* (2d. ed.). Englewood Cliffs, NJ: Prentice-Hall.

Ginott, H. G. (1961). *Group psychotherapy with children.* New York: McGraw-Hill.

Gitterman, A. (1989). Building mutual support in groups. *Social Work with Groups, 12* (2), 5–21.

Gitterman, A. & Shulman, L. (Eds.). (1986). *Mutual aid groups and the life cycle.* Itasca, IL: F. E. Peacock.

Glick, O. & Jackson, J. (1970). The effects of normative similarity on group formation of college freshmen. *Pacific Sociological Review, 13* (4), 263–269.

Goldstein, H. (1981). *Social learning and change: A cognitive approach to human services.* Columbia, SC: University of South Carolina Press.

Hare, A. P. (1962). *Handbook of small group research.* New York: Free Press.

Hartford, M. E. (1972). *Groups in social work.* New York: Columbia University Press.

Henry, S. (1992). *Group skills in social work.* (2d. ed.). Pacific Grove, CA: Brooks/Cole Publishing Co.

Herron, R. E. & Sutton-Smith, B. (1971). *Child's play.* New York: Wiley.

Hinchman, M. G. (1977). Clinical social work practice with children and youth: An analysis. Dissertation, University of Southern California.

Indelicato, S. & Goldberg, P. (1986). Harassed and alone: Parents of learning disabled children. In A. Gitterman & L. Shulman (Eds.), *Mutual aid groups and the life cycle* (pp. 195–209). Itasca, IL: F. E. Peacock.

Inhelder, B., & Piaget, J. (1958). *The growth of logical thinking from childhood to adolescence.* New York: Basic Books.

Johnson, C. (1974). Planning for termination of the group. In P. Glasser, R. Sarri

& R. Vinter (Eds.), *Individual change through small groups* (pp. 258–265). New York: The Free Press.

Kadushin, A. (1972). The racial factor in the interview. *Social Work, 17* (3), 88–98.

Katz, P. (1982). Development of children's racial awareness and intergroup attitudes. In L. Katz (Ed.), *Current topics in early childhood education* (Vol. 4). Norwood, NJ: Ablex.

Kohlberg, L. (1969). Stage and sequence: The cognitive-developmental approach to socialization. In D. S. Goslin (Ed.), *Handbook of socialization and research* (pp. 347–480). Chicago: Rand McNally.

Konopka, G. (1983). *Social group: A helping process* (3d. ed.). Englewood Cliffs, NJ: Prentice-Hall.

Kramer, S. & Rudolph, J. (1991). The latency stage. In S. I. Greenspan & G. H. Pollock (Eds.), *The course of life* (Vol. III, Middle and Late Childhood) (pp. 319–332). Madison, CT: International University Press.

Kurland, R. (1978). Planning: The neglected component of group development. *Social Work with Groups, 1* (2), 173–178.

Lee, J. A. B. & Swenson, C. R. (1986). The concept of mutual aid. In A. Gitterman & L. Shulman (Eds.), *Mutual aid groups and the life cycle* (pp. 361–380). Itasca, IL: F. E. Peacock.

Levine, B. (1979). *Group psychotherapy: Practice and development.* Englewood Cliffs, NJ: Prentice-Hall.

Lieberman, F. (1979). *Social work with children.* New York: Human Sciences Press.

Mahler, M. S. (1968). *On human symbiosis and the vicissitude of individuation.* New York: International Universities Press.

Mahler, M. S., Pine, F. & Bergman, A. (1975). *The psychological birth of the child: Symbiosis and individuation.* New York: Basic Books.

Maier, H. W. (Ed.). (1969). *Three theories of child development.* New York: Harper and Row.

McAdoo, H. (1977). Family therapy in the black community. *Journal of the American Orthopsychiatric Association, 47* (1), 75–79.

McGrath, J. & Altman, I. (1966). *Small group research: A synthesis and critique of the field.* New York: Holt, Rinehart & Winston.

Middleman, R. R., (1968). *The non-verbal method in working with groups.* New York: Association Press.

Middleman, R. R. & Wood, G. G. (1990). *Skills for direct practice in social work.* New York: Columbia University Press.

Minuchin, P. (1977). *The middle years of childhood.* Palo Alto, CA: Brooks/Cole.

Northen, H. (1969). *Social work with groups.* New York: Columbia University Press.

Northen, H. (1988). *Social work with groups* (2d. ed.). New York: Columbia University Press.

Ohrenstein, L. (1986). There is nothing latent about latency: Its impact on parents. *Child and Adolescent Social Work Journal, 3* (3), 143–150.

Olmsted, M. (1959). *The small group.* New York: Random House.

Overton, A. & Tinker, K. (1957). *Casework notebook.* St. Paul, MN: Greater St. Paul Community Chests and Councils.

Peller, L. E. (1978). *On development and education of young children.* New York: Philosophical Library.

Piaget, J. (1952). *The origins of intelligence in children*. New York: International University Press.

Piaget, J. (1969). *The mechanisms of perception*. New York: Basic Books.

Piaget, J. & Inhelder, B. (1969). *The psychology of the child*. New York: Basic Books.

Redl, F. (1944). Diagnostic group work. *American Journal of Orthopsychiatry, 14*, 53–67.

Redl, F. (1959). Strategy and technique of the life space interview. *American Journal of Orthopsychiatry, 29* (1), 1–18.

Redl, F. & Wineman, D. (1957). *The aggressive child*. New York: The Free Press.

Roberts, R. & Northen, H. (1976). *Theories of social work with groups*. New York: Columbia University Press.

Rosenberg, M. (1979). *Conceiving the self*. New York: Basic Books.

Sarnoff, C. A. (1980). Normal and pathological psychological development during the latency age period. In J. R. Bemporad (Ed.), *Child development in normality and psychopathology* (pp. 146–173). New York: Brunner/Mazel.

Sarnoff, C. A. (1987). *Pyschotherapeutic strategies in the latency years*. Northvale, NJ: Jason Aronson.

Sarri, R. & Galinsky, M. (1974). A conceptual framework for group work. In P. Glasser, R. Sarri & R. Vinter (Eds.), *Individual change through small groups* (pp. 71–88). New York: The Free Press.

Saywitz, K. (1987). Children's testimony: Age-related patterns of memory errors. In S. J. Ceci, M. P. Toglia & D. F. Ross (Eds.), *Children's eyewitness memory* (pp. 36–52). New York: Springer-Verlag.

Schaefer, C. E. (1980). Play therapy. In G. P. Sholevar, R. M. Benson & B. J. Binder (Eds.), *Emotional disorders in children and adolescents* (pp. 95–106). New York: Spectrum.

Schechter, M. D. & Combrink-Graham, L. (1991). In S. I. Greenspan & G. H. Pollock, *The course of life* (Vol. III, Middle and Late Childhood) (pp. 285–318). Madison, CT: International University Press.

Schwartz, W. (1971a). Social group work: The interactional approach. In *Encyclopedia of social work* (pp. 1253–1259). New York: National Association of Social Workers.

Schwartz, W. (1971b). On the use of groups in social work practice. In W. Schwartz & S. R. Zalba (Eds.), *The practice of group work* (pp. 2–24). New York: Columbia University Press.

Schwartz, W. (1974). The social worker in the group. In W. Klenk & R. M. Ryan (Eds.), *The practice of social work* (pp. 208–228). Belmont, CA: Wadsworth Publications.

Shaw, M. E. (1971) *Group dynamics: The psychology of small group behavior*. New York: McGraw-Hill.

Shulman, L. (1986). Group work method. In A. Gitterman & L. Shulman (Eds.), *Mutual aid groups and the life cycle* (pp. 23–51). Itasca, IL: F. E. Peacock.

Shulman, L. & Gitterman, A. (1986). The life model, mutual aid and the mediating function. In A. Gitterman & L. Shulman (Eds.), *Mutual aid groups and the life cycle* (pp. 3–22). Itasca, IL: F. E. Peacock.

Siepker, B. B. & Kandaras, C. S. (Eds.). (1985). *Group therapy with children and adolescents*. New York: Human Sciences Press.

Slavson, S. R. & Schiffer, M. (1975). *Group psychotherapy for children.* New York: International University Press.

Smalley, R. E. (1970). *Theories for social work practice.* New York: Columbia University Press.

Solomon, B. B. (1976). *Black empowerment: Social work in oppressed communities.* New York: Columbia University Press.

Sullivan, H. S. (1953). *The interpersonal theory of psychiatry.* New York: Norton.

Toseland, R. W. & Rivas, R. F. (1994). *An introduction to group work practice* (2d. ed.). Boston: Allyn and Bacon.

Trecker, H. B. (1948). *Social group work: Principles and practice.* New York: Women's Press.

Trieschmann, A. E., Whittaker, J. K. & Brendtro, L. K. (1969). *The other 23 hours.* Chicago: Aldine.

Vinter, R. D. (1974a). Program activities: An analysis of their effects on participant behaviors. In P. Glasser, R. Sarri & R. Vinter (Eds.), *Individual change through small groups* (pp. 233–243). New York: The Free Press.

Vinter, R. D. (1974b). An approach to group work practice. In P. Glasser, R. Sarri & R. Vinter (Eds.), *Individual change through small groups* (pp. 3–8). New York: The Free Press.

Vinter, R. D. (1974c). The essential components of social group work practice. In P. Glasser, R. Sarri & R. Vinter (Eds.), *Individual change through small groups* (pp. 9–33). New York: The Free Press.

Vinter, R. D. (1986a). Program activities: An analysis of their effects on participant behavior. In M. Sundel, P. Glasser, R. Sarri & R. Vinter (Eds.), *Individual change through small groups* (pp. 226–236). New York: The Free Press.

Ward, C. D. (1968). Seating arrangements and leadership emergence in small discussion groups. *Journal of Social Psychology, 74* (1), 83–90.

White, R. W. (1966). *Lives in progress* (2d. ed.). New York: Holt, Rinehart & Winston.

Whittaker, J. K. (1986). Program activities: Their selection and use in a therapeutic milieu. In M. Sundel, P. Glasser, R. Sarri & R. Vinter (Eds.), *Individual change through small groups* (pp. 237–250). New York: The Free Press.

Williams, M. (1972). Problems of technique during latency. *The Psychoanalytic Study of the Child, 37,* 598–620. New York: Quadrangle.

Wilson, G. (1976). From practice to theory: A personalized history. In R. Roberts & H. Northen (Eds.), *Theories of social work with groups* (pp. 1–44). New York: Columbia University Press.

Wilson, G. & Ryland, G. (1949). *Social group work practice.* Boston: Houghton-Miffin.

Yalom, I. D. (1985). *The theory and practice of group psychotherapy.* New York: Basic Books.

Zayas, L. H. & Lewis, B. H. (1986). Fantasy role-playing for mutual aid in children's groups: A case illustration. *Social Work with Groups, 9* (1), 53–66.

Index

About the Author

MARIAN F. FATOUT is the Betty J. Stewart endowed professor, School of Social Work, Louisiana State University. She has written extensively on social work issues.

ISBN 0-86569-256-4

HARDCOVER BAR CODE